Begin It Write

A Framework to Help Children to Acquire Written Language

CORNELIA STAATS

First published by Ultimate World Publishing 2023
Copyright © 2023 Cornelia Staats

ISBN

Paperback: 978-1-922982-68-1
Ebook: 978-1-922982-69-8

Cornelia Staats has asserted her rights under the Copyright, Designs and Patents Act 1988 to be identified as the author of this work. The information in this book is based on the author's experiences and opinions. The publisher specifically disclaims responsibility for any adverse consequences which may result from use of the information contained herein. Permission to use information has been sought by the author. Any breaches will be rectified in further editions of the book.

All rights reserved. No part of this publication may be reproduced, stored in or introduced into a retrieval system, or transmitted in any form, or by any means (electronic, mechanical, photocopying, recording or otherwise) without the prior written permission of the author. Any person who does any unauthorised act in relation to this publication may be liable to criminal prosecution and civil claims for damages. Enquiries should be made through the publisher.

Cover design: Ultimate World Publishing
Layout and typesetting: Ultimate World Publishing
Editor: Marinda Wilkinson
Cover Image Copyright: ImageFlow-Shutterstock.com

Ultimate World Publishing
Diamond Creek,
Victoria Australia 3089
www.writeabook.com.au

littera scripta manet

the written word remains

Contents

Introduction	1
Chapter 1: The Future Scene	5
Chapter 2: The Current Scene	11
Chapter 3: The Framework	21
Chapter 4: The Have to Have	31
Chapter 5: The Orthographic Code	39
Chapter 6: The Graphomotor Plan	51
Chapter 7: The Influences on Have to Have	69
Chapter 8: The Environment in Which I Live	75
Chapter 9: The Body & Brain I Inhabit	87
Chapter 10: The Dynamic System Perspective	99
Chapter 11: The Integration of Parts	105
Chapter 12: The Desire to Make a Difference	111
Afterword	117
Author Bio	119
Resources	121
Appendixes	125
Bibliography	135

Introduction

The purpose of this book is to provide a framework to help children acquire written language before they reach Year 2. The intended audience includes occupational therapists, classroom teachers, support staff and specialist professionals, with the global term 'educator' used to describe this group throughout. I have created terms to distinguish between skills that are crucial (Have to Have) and skills that exhibit ongoing development (Have to Grow) and have adopted the term 'influences' to describe social and biological factors that make it easier, or more difficult, to acquire written language.

Written language acquisition involves the mastery of two **Have to Have** skills:
- The orthographic code – alphabet knowledge and conceptual understanding of the alphabet principle
- The graphomotor plan – independent retrieval from memory and legible reproduction of alphabet letters.

To demonstrate achievement of this milestone, children must be able to read simple decodable text once they have mastered the alphabetic principle and can recognise visual words. They must independently and legibly write the 26 letters of the alphabet, from memory, within a specific time limit. For the vast majority of children, these abilities (and some beyond) are evident by the end of Year 1.

But there is strong evidence that a growing number of students are missing the mark.

Learning to handwrite is critical and should not be devalued. Neuroimaging studies show that the physical act of handwriting in children recruits brain regions associated with reading and strengthens letter recognition. Identifying letters is a strong predictor of early reading success. Mastery of handwriting letters facilitates learning to write text. There is a strong positive relationship between children's ability to read and write during the latter half of Foundation Year and first half of Year 1 – learning to handwrite helps children learn to read. Children are empowered when they learn that alphabetic symbols are abstractions for speech sounds and they can record their oral language by writing it down.

But handwriting is difficult to teach, difficult to learn, and requires dedication of both educator and child to acquire. Explicit handwriting instruction, and monitored handwriting practice, are necessary to achieve the worthy goal of independent retrieval and legible production of alphabet letters.

There is not one way to teach handwriting, just as there is not one way to teach reading. However, in order to handwrite and read, children must acquire distinct skills, or they will not progress – and for every child, there are influences that make acquiring these skills either easier, or more difficult.

While Have to Have skills may appear constrained – that is, there are a defined number of elements to be learnt and these can be

Introduction

mastered (Paris, 2005) – in contrast, reading comprehension is not constrained and can be expanded according to interest, exposure and instruction. Similarly, writing composition is not constrained; it involves spelling and constructing word sentences in legible handwriting. These abilities are defined in this book as **Have to Grow** skills to distinguish them from the Have to Have skills.

The distinction is important when considering written language acquisition, because too often, Have to Have and Have to Grow are confused. Concepts of print, identifying upper- and lower-case letters and letter-sound relations are constrained skills because the number of elements is small and finite. But once mastered, the realm of Have to Grow becomes more predictive of reading (and writing) progress. Both are necessary and overlap, but it matters what you do, and when you do it (Suggate, 2010).

Most children learn to read and write between the age of four and seven: a period of three years. This time frame constitutes a transition period when there is considerable intra-variability before the child reaches a state of stability. The state of stability occurs when changes in the cognitive system for reading and handwriting enable retrieval from long-term memory structures. Without these cognitive changes, variability continues. Intervention aims to reduce this variability.

The framework presented in this book is simple. It discusses the Have to Have skills (the orthographic code and graphomotor plan) in some detail and explains how they may be acquired. Influences that make acquisition either easier or more difficult are examined from the point of view of facilitator and detractor influences; they can either enhance or mitigate. Influences refer to environmental, and constitutional (body and brain) factors, unique to the child. In current times when everything has to happen 'now', there is also an appeal to respect the transition period, especially for the younger children in the class cohort.

Definitions and abbreviations are found in Appendix 1 and 2 at the back of the book. You will find free resources to access and additional opportunities to explore this subject further. Whether you are a teacher, occupational therapist, or support staff, I hope the information that follows is useful to consider, and critique, as you support children as they strive to acquire the written language.

CHAPTER 1

The Future Scene

As a nation, we have a collective responsibility to ensure that steps are taken to deliver on the educational goals for all young Australians. Any strategy requires a focus on both equity and excellence, supporting students from all backgrounds and communities to reach the highest levels of achievement. It must start from birth and address differences in need and opportunity across all stages of learning. While it may not be easy, it is critical that we set ourselves the task of achieving our national aspirations for education. Success can form the foundation of Australia's future prosperity, through generations of intelligent, confident, creative and engaged citizens.
Lamb, S., Huo, S., et.al., 2020

During Year 4, Stephen was referred for handwriting to students on clinical fieldwork placement. It took him four minutes to independently recall and handwrite 26 letters in lower case. The agreed goal for handwriting was line placement, but such goal would not only waste the boy's time but also the fieldwork students' time. A child in Year 4 who cannot independently recall and produce the 26 letters of the alphabet within a reasonable time frame does not have a line placement problem; he has a literacy problem.

A recent study (Lamb, 2020) reported that there are large numbers of learners missing out at each stage of the education system. At the time of school entry, 21.7% of children were not developmentally ready for school instruction. In the middle year, those missing national minimum standards had risen to 24.8% and by senior year 27.8% did not meet or exceed the international benchmark in mathematics, reading and science. By early adulthood, 29.7% were not in education, training or work. Amongst 24-year-olds, 38.1% were not actively engaged in the community.

Children's development in the early years can be a strong predictor of future achievement. The authors of the study suggest that the trajectory for meeting early (and later year) milestones tend to fall into four categories:
1. children initially succeeding who remain on track
2. children who are vulnerable but come back on track
3. children who started developmentally ready but subsequently fall behind
4. those children who were vulnerable and continue to struggle throughout their education.

Currently, the Australian education system is not doing so well to bridge these gaps in achievement. Children who experience social and financial disadvantage have the highest rate of school non-completion and underachievement. A recent report from the UNSW Gonski Institute for Education (Bonnor, 2021) stated:

The current Australian school system is concentrating disadvantaged students in disadvantaged schools, with serious implications for overall student achievement. This is a structural failure (p.11). The most opportunity for improving education quality is systematic structure reform.

Children who are at the highest risk of falling below the expected standards often have diverse or disadvantaged backgrounds, or reside in remote communities. However, there is evidence that children from at risk groups who are exposed to high expectations and systematic, explicit instruction gain a significant achievement boost. The point is, there will always be opportunities to make a difference, even in the face of adverse conditions.

The report also found that one in four children between the ages of five and 14 years were overweight or obese. Only 4% of children were meeting recommended guidelines for eating vegetables. Even more concerning is that 0.4% of children were homeless on Census night in 2016. This further reflects the resources (or lack of them) that the child brings to school.

What are the long-term costs of the problem continuing?

Cost to individual human wellbeing

Limited literacy negatively impacts self-concept and mental health because the cumulative effects are insidious. Not too long ago, if we were unable to fill out a form, then someone behind a counter would do it for us. Today, this is rare; we need to complete forms ourselves, usually online. The societal demands for literacy have increased, so the number of adults with limited literacy is of concern. Ironically in the digital age, we are constantly asked to agree to terms and conditions that even literate people find difficult to comprehend. Not unexpectedly this can be exploited to knowingly deceive people, which leads to desperate predicaments. Feelings of shame and worthlessness are reported by adults approaching volunteer services who support adult literacy development – and the impetus to seek assistance is often to be able to read to their own children.

Studies have demonstrated that juveniles in the justice detention system have significantly lower literacy achievement than their age peers. While family and social disadvantage may be contributing factors it is not difficult to imagine that being able to read and write from an early age could be a protective factor. Limited literacy may negatively impact access to some leisure pursuits.

Community economic cost and loss of productivity
If children fail early in their school years, they are more likely to disengage. Disengaged young people will struggle in the long term (more than half their adult life) to find work or go back into education. Lamb and Huo estimated that the cost to the government and the broader community of a person who does not engage in any work or education over most of their adult life is substantial (Lamb & Huo, 2017).

About 25% of Australian 24-year-olds are not actively engaged in work or education, namely, they are disengaged from the economic and social community. Many were early school leavers. Based on conservative modelling, it is estimated that for each disengaged person, the fiscal cost imposed is $411,700 across their adult years. The social costs are must higher. For each disengaged person, it is estimated they impose a cost of $1,103,700 across their lifetime (2017, p.8)

Every student, who fails to complete Year 12 or equivalent qualifications, or every young person who is not able to actively engage in work or study after they leave school, produces a direct cost on Australian taxpayers and government through lower tax revenues, higher dependence on public health and higher costs on crime and law enforcement systems (Lamb & Huo, 2017).

There is a real cost to the individual and the community when adults are not able to engage with the workplace. It is not only the loss of labour but also the loss of creativity and innovation. When young people do not engage in work or study, it negatively affects their opportunity to contribute to their society. There is less for re-distribution of wealth, including welfare, education and health services if the economic burden is exacerbated by high numbers of disengaged youth.

Limited literacy skills negatively impact employment opportunities. Work plays an important role in our lives. In some cases, people define themselves by the work that they do. 'What do you want to be when you grow up?' is a common question we ask children because work is bound up with our sense of wellbeing and self-essence.

Increasing inequality and civil unrest
Where there is increasing inequality of opportunity and outcome, there is often increasing unrest. In the last decade, the rise in populist movements in democracies has been attributed to the increasing gaps between those who have opportunities to be gainfully employed and earn sufficiently to look after their families and those who do not. The so-called knowledge workers are less affected by changes in economic downturns or world pandemics because they can work from anywhere, and many did work from home during the height of the pandemic. People who relied on customer/client contact were severely disenfranchised. Limited literacy is not the

only reason, but as societal demands for literacy increase, upheavals such as pandemics and economic downturns disproportionately negatively affect people with a history of literacy underachievement. Underachievement is also associated with behavioural problems, aggression, low self-esteem and depressive symptoms.

In summary

The future for children who do not achieve literacy standards to make academic progress is dire, not only for the individual but also for the community at large. While structural change may be difficult for educators to influence, it is possible to influence change at the educator-child interface.

This book offers a framework to clarify the 'what and when' for intervention, why it might be especially difficult for some children, and how to reframe the problem to move written language acquisition along. The following chapter presents the current drivers and deterrents to acquiring written language in the early years.

CHAPTER 2

The Current Scene

Written language is a cultural invention.
Colheart & Prior, 2007

Despite good intentions, every year there are children in Australia who leave Year 1 set up to fail. One of the reasons is because they have not learnt to read and write sufficiently to benefit from Year 2 and Year 3 instruction. By the end of Year 1, children have had two years of formal education. Although Australia has admirable goals for education, indicators for equal outcomes, inclusion and accessibility continue to deteriorate. Because poor readers and writers rarely catch up, it is important to get the foundations in place early. The National Assessment Program (NAPLAN) results show poor writing results in Year 3 tend to predict poor reading results in Year 5. The Australian education system compares well with global education systems, but it has a long tail of underachievement that continues to impact thousands of children. The solution offered is to go back to basics, which makes intuitive sense, but there is little explanation of what the basics are and why they work.

The Australian Curriculum (AC) was introduced to Australia in 2014. The term Foundation Year replaced previous terms to denote the school year before Year 1. At the time of writing, children must be five years old by 30 June of the current school year to commence primary school in most states of Australia, and they must be enrolled in school in the year they turn six. With some children entering the Foundation Year at age four, and some at six, there can be a large age gap between the oldest and youngest in the classroom.

While there is considerable attention paid to learning to read, there is less attention paid to learning to handwrite in the early years, despite writing being a valued outcome of early education. Writing and reading are integrally related, especially in the early years, and I propose in this book that there are two Have to Have (H2H) skills that children need to acquire written language: the **orthographic code** and the **graphomotor plan**. In the framework that follows I will explain what these are and why they are essential to written language acquisition.

Contributors to the problem

The vast majority of children learn to handwrite by the age of six or seven years old, but handwriting difficulties persist for between 10–30% of children. Longitudinal studies show that these children are also more likely to have reading difficulties (Katusic, 2009). Handwriting difficulties that persist are concerning and current societal trends contribute to this problem.

Handwriting is devalued

Although there is lip service paid to handwriting, it is generally not considered as important a skill as it was previously. This began with the introduction of the typewriter, followed by the desktop computer. Today, it would be rare for adults to do most of their writing by hand; instead many would use a word processor.

> *How important is handwriting? It is very important.*
> **Ediger, 2002**

Increased screen time

It has become almost cliché to say that children indulge in too much screen time. Time spent on screen is time *not* spent on learning to use your hands in the 3D space. Children need physical interaction in play with various objects of different textures and weights. Tool use in the form of spades, paint brushes, pencils, eating utensils and scissors prepares sensory-motor pathways that underpin later motor performance. Handwriting involves the use of tools and operating in a space away from self.

The introduction of iPads in the mid-2000s was seen as an opportunity to increase children's creativity. The technology was introduced into schools with relatively little thought about the possible negative consequences. Most of the commentary around that time was about the positive elements it would bring to the classroom. The problem with screen time is that for the most part, it is a consumption device, not a creative device, especially for children in the early years. It is a myth that screen learning is the same as classroom learning as we witnessed in the COVID pandemic, which exposed the inherent misconceptions about the usefulness of online learning.

Screen time can be broadly summarised as any screen: television, iPads, computer and consoles. The majority of Australian children exceed recommendations for screen time (Tooth, 2019).

Compared to other countries, Australian classrooms have the highest proportion of children using digital devices, including computers, in school. We are the highest users of technology. An OECD report (OECD, 2015) stated that iPads in school do not improve literacy and numeracy. Even though the report acknowledges the importance of learning to navigate the digital world, it stressed that students need to be equipped with basic literacy and numeracy skills to fully participate in the 21st century.

There is also a proliferation of aids that help those who have difficulty with literacy such as speech-to-text and text-to-speech. Perversely, this may lead to unconscious bias to reduce the importance and necessity of achieving written language in the early years. Competent adults forget that their ability to use a word processor is based on their conceptual understanding of the alphabetic symbols on the keyboard and what they mean for communication. The predicted demise of handwriting is grossly misunderstood and exaggerated.

Crowded curriculum
The school is seen as a place where any social issue can be targeted because the students are a captive audience. Increasingly, school is not seen as only important for numeracy and literacy but as a preparation for 'effective personhood' for the complex world they will live in (Hickey, 2021). Given we don't know exactly what world students will live in, it seems that consolidating literacy and numeracy could be a more useful place to start.

Especially in the early years, insufficient time allocated to repetitive cycles of the same material and spaced practice to consolidate what is being taught becomes disproportionately disadvantageous. Educators need time to engage with the evaluative judgement of children's work to identify the gaps in knowledge that need to be repeated and practised. In addition to literacy and numeracy, the AC wishes to address information technology capability, critical and creative thinking, personal and social capability, ethical understanding and intercultural understanding at every year level.

Children are more vulnerable
The Australian Early Development Index (AEDI) is a national assessment to assess how children have developed by the time they start school. Their findings are disturbing (AEDC, 2021).

Today, at least 22% of children are considered vulnerable and so they are 'less' ready for school. This is a red flag for educators as they can anticipate that some children in every classroom will need additional support. The apparent increase in child vulnerability is occurring at the same time the expectations of what children are supposed to achieve academically are increasing. The response of most English-speaking countries is similar – to start earlier. There appears to be great panic about not getting there quickly. However, rushing does not seem to be the answer. Countries that start later, such as Finland, Sweden and Korea rank higher than Australia in reading tables published by the Programme in the International Student Assessment (PISA) achievement tables (OECD, 2018). To be a failure at the end of Year 1 has obvious negative consequences. Age also makes a difference but unfortunately, there is no disentanglement of ability from maturity. The youngest child in any classroom is already at risk if expectations are the same as for the oldest child in the class (Whitely, 2021).

Post-COVID, the data collection for the 2021 AEDI showed that the percentage of children on track, those with no identifiable developmental vulnerability, had decreased from 55.4% in 2018 to 54.8% in 2021. Consequently, there was an increase in the number of children who demonstrated developmental vulnerability. Those vulnerable in one domain increased from 21.7% in 2018 to 22% in 2022, and those vulnerable in two or more domains increased from 11% in 2018 to 11.4% in 2022.

The language and cognitive school-based domain showed the most significant increase of children developmentally vulnerable from 6.6% in 2018 to 7.3% in 2021. The physical health and wellbeing domain and the emotional maturity domain showed a small increase in vulnerability in 2021. Gains that had been made in communication skills and general knowledge were not sustained during the pandemic and there was an increase in vulnerability from 8.2% in 2018 to 8.4% in 2021. These figures are important because they give us some insight into the resources (or not) that the child brings to school. Highly relevant for educators is that just under a quarter of the children entering school will demonstrate at least one developmental vulnerability.

The proliferation of specialists in schools
Health and education services are not well integrated in Australia, for the most part, operating independently of one another. This means that children between four and seven years of age who are not progressing as expected at school are often referred to allied health for intervention with questionable opportunities for collaboration between the two environments. Allied health services include occupational therapy, speech therapy, physiotherapy, exercise physiology and behaviour support.

The introduction of occupational therapists, speech therapists and psychologists in schools is generally considered to be a good thing, but they are a response to a problem. The increased use of services is linked to many more children with vulnerabilities entering school. While helpful, there is potential for conflict around competing aims, so unless there is good communication, it may be counterproductive. In addition, children receiving the specialised service may end up receiving less instruction time in class which can disadvantage them further. There may be little transfer because what the specialist is working on is not directly relatable to the classroom. The extra time taken for consultation and documentation becomes an additional burden when there are competing goals. Where it works well is when health and education professionals have time to consult as a multidisciplinary team to support children.

Confusion about Have to Have vs Have to Grow skills
This book makes a distinction between the **Have to Have** (H2H) skills, which are the orthographic code and the graphomotor plan, and **Have to Grow** (H2G) skills. The H2H skills are basic to written language acquisition and must be mastered within a limited time, while the H2G skills continue to develop over time.

The Australian English curriculum has three strands: (i) language: knowing about the English language, (ii) literature: understanding, appreciating, responding to, analysing and creating literary text, and (iii) literacy: expanding the repertoire of English usage.

The achievement standards list H2G and H2H knowledge and skills together (see below), which potentially underestimates how much the acquirement of H2H skills influences a child's ability to progress. Of course, it is good and necessary to expose children to H2G knowledge and skills while they acquire H2H skills because they are all related. However, the issue with the H2H skills is that they are acquired within a limited time, while H2G skills are open-ended and can develop over time.

The following is taken from the Australian Curriculum (version 8.4) Achievement Standard for Foundation Year students:
- Reads short, decodable and predictable texts
- Recognises and names English alphabet letters, in upper and lower case and uses the most common sounds represented by most letters
- Reads high-frequency words and blends sounds orally to read consonant vowel consonant words
- When writing uses familiar words and phrases and images to convey ideas
- Writing shows evidence of letter and sound knowledge, beginning writing behaviours, experimentation with capital letters and full stops
- Correctly forms **known** upper- and lower-case letters.

Achievement Standard for Year 1 students:
- When reading, uses knowledge of the relationship between letters and sounds, high-frequency words, sentence boundary punctuation and directionality to make meaning
- When writing, students provide details about ideas or events, and details about participants in those events
- Accurately spells high-frequency words and words with regular spelling patterns
- Uses capital letters and full stops and forms **all** upper- and lower-case letters correctly.

The H2H skills that relate directly to the framework are phonics and word knowledge, and consolidating legible handwriting. The descriptions of what they mean in the AC are listed below.

Phonics and word knowledge: *Students develop knowledge about the sounds of English (phonemes) and learn to identify the sounds in spoken words. They learn the letters of the alphabet (graphemes)* and how to represent spoken words by using combinations of these letters. The application of phonemic awareness and phonic knowledge to the development of reading especially from Foundation Year to Year 2 is of critical importance.

Creating text: *Students develop and consolidate a handwriting style that is legible, fluent and automatic, and that supports sustained writing.*

A curriculum is designed to sequence an educational programme. Learning to read has received more attention than learning to handwrite: *application of phonemic awareness and phonic knowledge to the development of reading especially from Foundation Year to Year 2 is of critical importance.* What is absent in the AC is identifying what is critically important to develop and consolidate a legible handwriting style.

In summary

The vast majority of children read and write before they enter Year 2, but Australia has a long tail of underachievement. This book promotes the view that learning to handwrite is just as important as learning to read for children to acquire written language. This chapter presented some barriers to achieving this goal.

The following chapter presents a framework to help children to acquire written language.

CHAPTER 3

The Framework

Sesame Street has run for more than 30 years. Children today know their numbers and letters earlier than ever before. Many know them by age two. Yet children today are not learning math or reading any earlier or better than did children before there was Sesame Street.
Elkind in Elkind & Whitehurst, 2001

I have yet to meet a student with fluent handwritten language that has problems reading.
Jones, 2004

I have been influenced by some fads in my working life and I am probably not alone. Fads usually illuminate some interesting aspect related to the subject but they are rarely the whole picture. I don't know how many 'evidence-based' phonics courses I went to, but there were more than a few. I attended a number of workshops on handwriting. One, related to sensory motor techniques, used corrugated cardboard to write letters, another wooden sticks and curves, yet another wooden shapes but with different colours to distinguish between them. All presenters were sincere in their approach and they were successful in helping children achieve their goals. But as any course attendee knows, the transition from translating content to practice is not always automatic. One of the reasons, I believe, is that presenters have tacit knowledge that is not immediately obvious to the course attendee but it is integral to the presenter's approach. We all operate from a belief system about teaching handwriting or learning to read that we may not even be aware of: it is our personal theory of written language. The framework presented in this chapter, and subsequent chapters predicated on the framework, is my personal theory. It may, or may not, resonant with what you believe to be true. It is open to critique and rebuttal, but hopefully will help readers clarify their own personal theory of written language acquisition.

The importance of the early years is well documented. This is especially true for literacy and numeracy as these skills form part of a basic education. The Australian Curriculum (8.4) stresses that *'the application of phonemic awareness and phonic knowledge to the development of reading, especially from Foundation to Year 2, is of critical importance'*. However, when it comes to writing, the AC is vague as to time lines and importance. The expectation is that children *will consolidate a handwriting style that is legible, fluent and automatic, and that supports sustained writing.* Handwriting is not the only means listed for what children will use to demonstrate what they know – the use of drawing, digital text and presentation are mentioned as alternatives. At the Foundation Year level children are expected to produce **some** lower- and upper-case letters using common letter formation, so their ability to self-generate text is limited. By the end of Year 1, the expectation is increased that they will use capital letters and full stops and form **all** upper- and lower-case letters correctly, so their ability to self-generate text is anticipated.

While there is an acknowledgement that learning to read can take at least two to three years, there is not the same acknowledgement for handwriting. Yet there is increasing evidence that reading and writing are integrally related (Bear, 2008), and longitudinal studies support the relationship between writing ability and reading ability (Abbott, Berninger, & Fayol, 2010).

At this stage of children's development, learning to handwrite in order to generate text also takes time. Neural changes in cognitive architecture need to take place for children to read and handwrite (Dehaene, 2009).

The Have to Have skills

In this chapter, I explain the difference between Have to Have (H2H) skills, which are foundations or 'the basics' for acquiring written language, and Have to Grow (H2G) skills, which are necessary to progress written language capabilities.

Early models of cognitive architecture proposed a two-component model for processing information, namely, long-term memory and short-term memory. Input from the environment was processed in short-term memory before being stored in long-term memory; the notion of short-term memory was later revised to be replaced by a multi-component system termed working memory (Baddeley, Hitch, & Allen, 2019).

According to the Baddeley & Hitch model, working memory is a limited-capacity system that allows temporary storage and manipulation of information for complex cognitive tasks. The components of the working memory system are the central executive and two subsidiary systems:
- the phonological loop, which holds speech-based information
- the visuospatial sketchpad for visual information.

The central executive controls *what* gets attention and has no capacity for storage. The visuospatial memory in typically developing children can be separated into memory for spatial information and memory for visual information. For our purposes, we have long-term memory (LTM), and working memory (WM) with limited capacity, but we are able to link and hold visual and speech-based information for a brief time. To read and write, structures must be laid down in long-term memory. The best way to accommodate a limited WM is to build stronger links and connections in LTM; this takes time and the child must be actively engaged in this process. In the early years, the child's reading performance is directly controlled by the cognitive architecture for carrying out reading, and the child's writing performance is directly controlled by the cognitive architecture for carrying out handwriting (Colheart, 2017).

The notion that phonemes exist is the result of alphabetisation (Dehaene, 2009). Illiterate people are unable to, or have great difficulty, in isolating phonemes. Knowing grapheme-phoneme correspondence and understanding how it works is a H2H skill. Initial explicit, systematic phonics instruction is necessary to acquire reading. If you know the direct letter-sound correspondence of the 26 letters of the alphabet and can manipulate them (a constrained skill), then it is easier to understand the exceptions. Now the child can build stronger and more elaborate memory structures in cognitive architecture progressing from H2H skills to H2G skills.

The Framework

Instruction moves beyond phonics to develop reading fluency and comprehension. These H2G abilities are unconstrained, open-ended, and continue to advance throughout life according to study and interest.

The role of alphabet knowledge is often undervalued for the conceptual understanding of phonemic awareness, which in turn contributes to the alphabetic principle. Children perceive the alphabetic principle when they access systematic letter-sound relationships to read or pronounce unfamiliar words. The orthographic code is critical to the framework for acquiring written language and is here defined as both alphabet knowledge and conceptual understanding of the alphabetic principle. In addition to the orthographic code, the graphomotor plan is critical to the framework for acquiring written language. The dual function of alphabet knowledge in the orthographic code and the graphomotor plan will become obvious. The graph, an abstract symbol to represent speech sound, is central to both.

To handwrite, children must have a mental representation of the letter/s to recall it.

A multicomponent cognitive network that incorporates what the letter looks like, the sound it represents, and the spatial parameters of how to form its characteristic shape is built up in LTM over time. Handwriting is a particular kind of motor skill because there are no environmental spatial targets for movement when handwriting a letter (Overvelde, 2013). In contrast to other learned movements, it is not the end result but the shape of the movement trajectory for forming a letter/s that is crucial.

Explicit, systematic instruction is necessary to learn the spatial parameters that organise the letter shape. The child recalls from memory the letter and learns by their conscious effort the spatial sequence that includes orientation of each letter. With sufficient practice, judicial instructor feedback and self-evaluation, the conscious spatial sequencing is replaced by an internal representation of the motor sequence: the graphomotor plan. The graphomotor plan must be independently retrieved to reproduce the distinctive features of a letter/s when writing composition.

The graphomotor plan is a H2H skill and learning the spatial parameters for each letter is a constrained skill because the maximum number of letters and their distinctive features to learn is 52. The independent retrieval of both upper and lower case for each letter, and its handwritten reproduction according to legibility conventions is necessary to write self-generated text.

We do not expect children to just write the alphabet letters according to their characteristic shape; rather we expect them to reproduce them to make meaning through writing. The independent retrieval of the graphomotor plan enables the child to build upon their existing cognitive architecture and progress from H2H skills to H2G skills – writing for meaning using appropriate text structure, vocabulary, spelling and grammar. It is important to note that H2H and H2G learning overlap and H2G learning takes place while H2H is consolidated.

Figure 1 displays the overlap between the orthographic code and the graphomotor plan. In the framework, these two are considered essential for written language acquisition. They are the H2H skills and are generally achieved between the age of four to seven years when children receive explicit, systematic instruction.

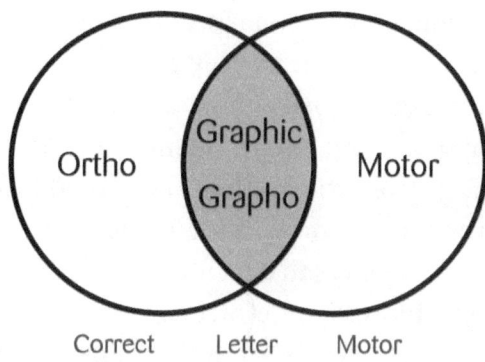

Figure 1. The Have to Have knowledge and skills

The role of influences

The acquisition of written language in cognitive architecture should be viewed developmentally. Before the role of influences is introduced, an analogy of a building may be helpful. Early development is concerned with setting up foundations for the (cognitive) building: oral language, sensory-motor play, being read to, immersed in print-rich environments, fine motor manipulations, learning to self-regulate in social environments, word games, singing nursery rhymes, drawing pictures and other activities positively correlated with acquiring literacy. The building bricks are usually assembled before the child goes to school. By the time the child enters school they are ready to benefit from the mortar (explicit, systematic instruction, feedback and practice) to hold these bricks in place. Sometimes the mortar is a bit sloppy so it takes more time to set, or it needs more cement. The mortar has to be set around networks connecting visual, speech and motor bodies of knowledge. These bodies of knowledge contribute to cementing the H2H – orthographic code and graphomotor plan – in LTM. Most children build this cognitive architecture between the age of four to seven years.

Sometimes these bricks do not end up in the correct place because of social and environmental differences, and/or biological and genetic differences. This does not mean they can't be moved later, but it takes more effort. How effortful it is to acquire written language is influenced by social and environmental, and/or biological and genetic differences. Collectively, they are termed influences in the framework. Influences can facilitate or detract from acquiring written language. Influences that facilitate are labelled as Facilitator Influence (FI) and those that detract as Detractor Influence (DI). They are discussed in more detail in the following chapters.

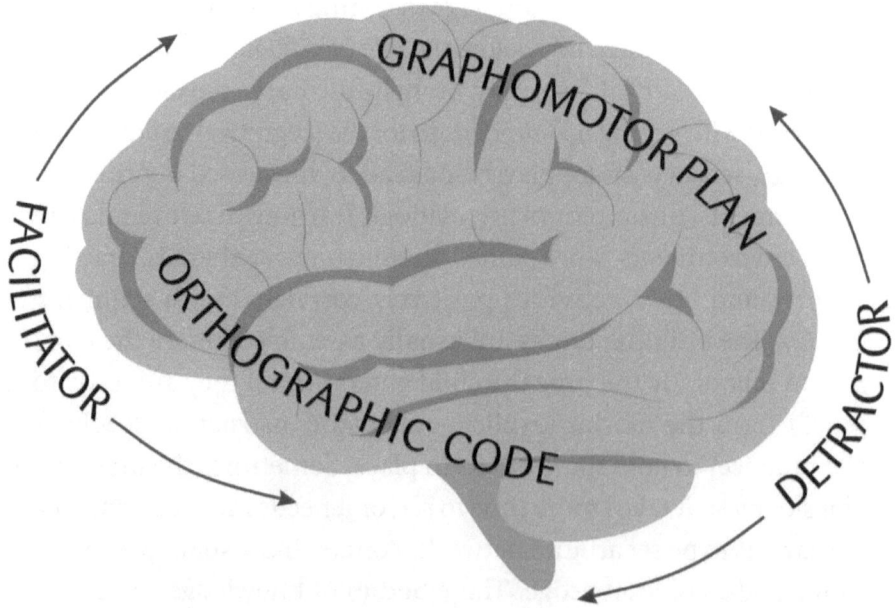

Figure 2. A conceptual model of the framework

Figure 2 depicts the H2H skills as embedded in cognitive architecture. The influences can either facilitate or detract from this process. Therefore, how easy or difficult the acquisition of written language is for the child should always be viewed in the context of their individual differences and their social circumstances.

In summary

This chapter presented an overview of the framework. The orthographic code and the graphomotor plan share **graph**, the letter symbol; there is an interactive and dynamic relationship between the code and the plan that is mediated through the letter. There are influences, environmental and biological/genetic, which either support this relationship or detract from it.

The following chapter will briefly review the necessary H2H skills the child must master in order to acquire written language: the orthographic code and the graphomotor plan.

CHAPTER 4

The Have to Have

> *The written word may be man's greatest invention.*
> *It allows us to converse with the dead, the absent,*
> *and the unborn.*
> **Abraham Lincoln**

Sally loved to play with different colours from an early age. At four years old, she was drawing and colouring in pictures of her family and scenes from stories and everyday events with some sophistication. She enjoyed cutting out pictures and pasting them on cards, signing her name with a flourish.

In contrast, Simon at age four years, hated to draw and was even less interested in colouring inside the lines. Cutting was a nightmare and the most 'boring' activity ever. He was more interested in riding his scooter and building ramps in the backyard. He loved being read to and enjoyed acting out superhero stories. He recognised 'S' for Simon but had no interest in reproducing it.

When they both entered Foundation Year, Sally progressed steadily from drawing and understanding that her 'S' represented her name but also that it represented the sound /s/ as in snake and swing. She found alliterative phrases such as silly snake highly amusing. By the end of the year, she was handwriting her entire name, as well as many other letters of the alphabet, consistently and legibly. In contrast, Simon spent most of the first half of the year perfecting his drawing of a scooter, or variations thereof, as a substitute for writing activities. He became interested in writing his name when it was pointed out that /s/ is the beginning sound, and letter, for scooter and Simon. It took a while longer for Simon than for Sally, but by the end of Year 1, he had progressed steadily from drawing scooters to handwriting letters.

The parallels between the historical progression of written language and children's progression from initial scribbles through to representational drawings and finally handwriting are interesting. Written language is a very sophisticated technology. It took millennia to develop to its present form as an alphabet of 26 letters for writing in English. The history of writing probably began with simple drawings, some of which still exist today. Over time, these drawings became more complex. Initially, simple drawings that represented objects or persons (pictograms) bore no connection to oral language, but later pictograms were extended to represent ideas (ideograms). A paradigmatic shift occurred when ideograms began to represent sounds of the language.

The first known syllabic system, cuneiform writing, was developed by the Sumerians. The Greeks turned to cuneiform writing but they found it was an inefficient system because the Greek language has a complex syllable structure. Instead, the Greeks borrowed the Phoenician writing system that used phonograms to represent individual sounds of the language. The result was the alphabetic writing system where typically one symbol or group of symbols represents one sound unit or phoneme. The Romans (Latins) adopted this writing system around the 7th century BC; after many iterations, this has culminated in the alphabet used in English today. The capital letters of the English alphabet are Latin script, but these symbolic representations remain a cypher if you do not have the code. The code gives access to what they mean.

The orthographic code

The code, which for the purposes of this framework is included under the umbrella term **orthographic code**, is that every alphabet letter symbol or combination of alphabet letter symbols can be mapped to a speech sound of the language. The letter(s) are called **graphemes** and the sounds are called **phonemes**. Graphic variation in font, size and/or capitalisation does not affect a letter's identity. The H2H skill is to 'crack the code' for these 26 letters. However, English has approximately 40–44 phonemes depending on regional differences in accent, so alphabet letters need to be combined as stable units to represent these additional sounds. Children progress to the realm of H2G skills when they build on their initial knowledge of the code. By definition, children need access to the alphabet if they are to crack the code.

Learning to recite the alphabet and increasing alphabet knowledge contributes to understanding the code. However, singing the alphabet song is just that, singing a song, and many children have no idea that *elmnop* is five distinct letters sung as one word. This does not mean there are no children who learn the alphabet through the song. Some do, but it cannot be assumed. Alphabet knowledge (letter recognition, letter name, letter sound, upper case, lower case) is a unidimensional construct that shows a developmental progression achieved over time (Drouin, 2012).

Regular grapheme-phoneme (letter-sound) patterns are learnt initially (H2H) and later learning extends to irregular patterns (H2G). Patterns of direct letter-sound correspondence are sometimes referred to as the initial code and patterns of letter combinations for one sound or one letter representing different sounds are sometimes referred to as the extended code. Exposure and mastery of the initial code helps children to consolidate the alphabetic principle as they consistently and accurately map the speech sound to the alphabet letter/s and vice versa. This enables them to decode the sounds of a group of letters, for example, the word c/a/t, and synthesise or blend these individual letters, c/a/t, to read the word 'cat'. Neuroimaging studies show that learning to read changes the brain (Dehaene, 2009). Mastering the orthographic code is a H2H skill and necessary to lay strong foundations in memory structures for written language. The extended code is a H2G skill that continues to build on this foundation and in so doing increase children's proficiency and enjoyment of written language.

Handwriting in an alphabetic system is the motor reproduction of symbols representing the speech sounds of oral language. Learning to handwrite letters draws attention to speech sounds and attention to speech sounds refines the understanding of the letter symbol; it is an interactive and dynamic relationship.

The graphomotor plan

The developmental progression of our writing system appears to be stable; from markings to representational drawings to symbols, that is, from concrete to abstract. We can recognise it in children's development before they enter school. They start with marking the paper with indiscriminate scribbles, before moving on to drawings that become more representational as they mature. They may write some numbers before letters; often the number four is the first number they recognise on their birthday cards. They may even be able to write their name before they enter school. Children may be able to do all that and not understand the alphabetic principle. They have yet to move from a concrete to an abstract symbolic system.

Learning to handwrite independently requires access to the orthographic code. It is possible to copy text and have no idea what it means. The aim of instruction is that children are able to independently recall, retrieve and reproduce these abstract symbols to make meaning through written language to be read by self and others.

To acquire written language, in addition to the orthographic code, children must master the graphomotor plan. Children receive explicit and systematic instruction in, and are required to practise, letter formations according to social conventions of legibility to ensure these symbols retain their value as written communication. The length and duration of instruction and practice must be sufficient for children in order to independently retrieve, from LTM, letters during writing tasks. Writing words and sentences, which are H2G skills, are predicated on this independent retrieval of the graphomotor plan for the letter. Handwriting must access a stable graphomotor plan and maintain a bidirectional relationship with the orthographic code, to demonstrate written language.

Explicit and systematic instruction

The majority of children do not learn to acquire the orthographic code and the graphomotor plan without explicit and systematic instruction.

Explicit instruction, sometimes termed direct instruction, implies an intentional approach. Systematic indicates a logical sequence of instruction to address what needs to be taught about a given topic. Where instructors begin in the sequence depends on the children. Some children come from print-rich environments, but some do not. The mantra, 'I do, We do, You do' takes notice of where the child is at and helps educators step into the appropriate sequence from that point to inform instruction.

The following list provides an overview of what effective explicit instruction entails.
- Begin a lesson by activating prior knowledge.
- Present new material in small steps, with the child practising after each step. Limit the number of materials children receive at one time.
- Give clear and detailed instructions and explanations.
- Ask a large number of questions and check for understanding.
- Provide a high level of active practice with many examples for all children. Guide them as they begin to practise.
- Use think-aloud and model steps.
- Ask children to explain what they have learned (see interleaving for handwriting).
- Check the responses of all children.
- Provide systematic feedback and corrections.
- Reteach material when necessary.
- Prepare children for independent practice.
- Monitor children when they begin independent practice (also known as dynamic monitoring) (Rosenshine, 2012).

For procedural learning like handwriting, the best practice is spaced repetition, 10–15 minutes at least three times a week, and interleaving. An example of interleaving may be a handwriting lesson followed by the educator using a think-aloud protocol to spell words and/or sentences on the board with presented and practised letters in the previous lesson. When introducing a science topic word on the board, the educator may ask 'how do I start that letter again?' 'OK, where do I go next?' 'Which way does it go again?' and so on. The think-aloud protocol can be used anytime for relevant topic words thus presenting another opportunity for children to retrieve verbal cues from memory.

The time frame

At the end of Year 1, which is two years of formal instruction in school, the AC expects children to have mastered the knowledge of sound-letter correspondence of alphabet letters and the ability to correctly form upper- and lower-case letters. This framework supports these expectations because they are H2H skills. Children can use their letter-sound knowledge to independently read decodable text. Children can independently retrieve and handwrite correctly formed upper- and lower-case letters of the alphabet.

Give me six hours to chop down a tree, and I will spend the first four sharpening the axe.
Abraham Lincoln

In summary

This chapter provided a brief overview of the H2H skills: the orthographic code and the graphomotor plan. Because the **graph** is so important, the alphabet is important.

The following chapter discusses in more detail the contribution of alphabet knowledge to the orthographic code.

A helpful chart to illustrate the progression from proto-semitic to Latin script can be found at: https://sbltn.com/labnotes/evolutionofthealphabet

CHAPTER 5

The Orthographic Code

*The learning of alphabet letters is a major
landmark in alphabetic literacy acquisition.*
Foulin, 2005

To date, I have met very few children referred for handwriting who were able to recite the alphabet sequence without error. Every time I say that people look at me as if I do not know what I am talking about. The alphabet song is so ubiquitous that it seems incredible children do not know how to recite the alphabet. Maybe recitation of the alphabet is insufficiently valued as an important contributor to acquiring written language, and/or is rarely assessed. But educators should listen carefully to children reciting the alphabet as they may make naming errors such as <eks> for <es>, or <bee> for <vee>.

These errors appear minor, but they are errors that may interfere with letter recognition and/or initial letter-sound correspondences. It cannot be assumed that children know the alphabet when they enter school, even though they may sing the alphabet song. Assessing for alphabet knowledge is the first place to look if children are not progressing as expected.

Although seemingly easy, it turns out that acquiring alphabet knowledge is a complex, abstract task for young children to achieve. Complete and total mastery of all alphabet letters is a universal prerequisite for children to make progress in reading and writing because alphabet knowledge is the single best predictor of later reading and writing success, even though its influence may be indirect (Reutzel, 2015). The foundation for the orthographic code is the alphabet.

The alphabet is unidimensional

Alphabet knowledge is a unitary construct, but it follows a developmental progression of overlapping proficiency. Alphabet knowledge is everything we know about the alphabet: recognition of letters, naming letters, mapping sounds to letters, and identifying the difference between upper and lower case. In other words, these are not different knowledges, but they are one and the same. To test this assumption, Drouin and colleagues conducted a study with 335 children, aged between four and five years, using the Rasch model (Drouin, 2012). Analysing data with the Rasch model places the test items aligned with children's performance on the same scale; test results are distributed along an ability continuum, rather than distributed around the average score. Test data must fit the requirements of the Rasch model. Easier items are achieved by children with less ability and harder items by children with more ability.

There were four tests of alphabet knowledge administered where the child had to respond after the assessor pointed, in random order, to individual letters:
1. lower-case letters of different fonts named by the child
2. upper-case letters named by the child
3. letter sounds of upper-case letters named by the child
4. upper case recognition of letters named by the assessor.

For each of the four tests, children were asked to point to the letter. All 26 upper-case letters were displayed in random order on a separate six-item page. Tasks were administered in the order listed. Scoring was 0 or 1: either the child did or did not know the answer. Upon completion of data analysis, these findings emerged. There is a developmental progression for alphabet knowledge, and most of the alphabet tasks overlap; it begins with letter recognition, followed by upper case naming, then lower case naming, and finally, letter sounds. Older children achieved the more difficult items compared to younger children.

Given that alphabet knowledge is developmental, repetitive cycles of instruction would appear to be necessary.

Enhanced alphabet knowledge

In the article titled, *N is for Nonsensical*, the author reports on a lesson observation where the letter N was presented in a variety of ways for 55 minutes (Neuman, 2006). Each week another letter was tackled in the same way. The author noted that at a rate of one letter per week, it would take 26 weeks to complete the alphabet, and by then the children may have forgotten the first letters presented. According to neuroscientist Stanislas Dehaene, the goal of early literacy instruction is to lay down an efficient neuronal hierarchy in our brain so that a child can recognise letters (graphemes) and easily turn them into speech sounds (phonemes). For these neural connections to stabilise and strengthen children must revisit the same information through many hours, days and months for the consolidation process to progress.

One of the biggest reasons that children between ages five to six years do not learn to read as well as their peers is because they do not know the alphabet (Jones, 2012). As literate people we understand phonemes exist because of alphabetisation. This may seem contentious to some, but whether the letters or sounds come first is really a chicken and egg problem. That letters are an abstraction for speech sounds requires a letter symbol to which we attribute this property.

But because repetitive cycles are necessary to consolidate neural connections, alphabet instruction can seem boring. Jones (2012) identified six avenues that she termed **advantages** to help children remain interested while presenting the entire alphabet through multiple cycles. The name of her programme is Enhanced Alphabet Knowledge.

The Enhanced Alphabet Knowledge (EAK) advantages that inform the cycles are:
- own name advantage based on the frequency order of the first letter in children's names e.g. four children have names beginning with A, two children have names beginning with J and so on
- the sequential order of the alphabet
- letter name-sound relationships based on the acrophonic principle where the letter name corresponds to the letter sound e.g. B for bee. Other letters follow the acrophonic principle for initial phonemes (consonant-vowel names) e.g.

b[ee], d, p, or as final phoneme (vowel-consonant name) e.g. [e]f, l, m, n, r, s
- letter frequency based on letter frequency in environmental print
- the general order of developmental consonant phoneme acquisition
- distinguishing visual features of letters in written forms; emphasis placed on the critical distinctive features between similar letters.

Each advantage forms the basis of an instruction cycle. Each cycle consisted of one letter per day, five per week, and followed the same explicit lesson format with teacher modelling and guided practice.

The lessons are daily and brief (12–15 minutes) with three components: identifying the letter name and sound, recognising the letter in a text and producing the letterform.

EAK lessons teach the name and sound of both upper- and lower-case forms for each letter. There are at least six cycles of alphabet instruction in one school year, which allows time for an additional cycle to revisit problem letters.

Alphabet knowledge includes letter names

There is a longstanding debate about the function of letter names in reading. In Great Britain letter names are not routinely taught, so clearly, letter name knowledge is not a prerequisite for learning letter sounds. However, there are three main benefits of knowing letter names to acquire written language:

1. it supports phonological processing of print e.g. children often associate meaning to the first letter of their name before they have any idea about the alphabetic principle
2. it supports learning letter-sound correspondence, in particular for letters that follow the acrophobic principle
3. as preparation for learning grapheme-phoneme correspondences (Foulin, 2005).

According to Foulin (2005), 'the assumption appears fairly safe that letter name knowledge, with early phonological awareness skills such as onset-rime segmentation […], assists children's self-discovery of the alphabetic principle'. In other words, if children do not discover the alphabetic principle by themselves, then the assumption appears fairly safe that they are at least primed to benefit from instruction because they know the name of the letter/s that represent sound.

Alphabet knowledge on its own is not enough; phonics instruction is needed

Reading to your children does not guarantee that your child will learn to read and write easily, as caregivers have found to their chagrin, but it helps. Alphabet knowledge, on the other hand, is a predictor of reading and writing because it lays the foundation in cognitive architecture (LTM) for a conceptual understanding of the alphabetic principle (Reutzel, 2015) when paired with phonics instruction.

There are many structured and systematic phonics programmes, but they are not all the same. It depends on the conceptual framework adopted by the authors. Some examples are Jolly Phonics, Sounds-Write, Alpha to Omega, Sound Waves and Words Their Way to name a few. Many schools have a preference for one programme over another. Most phonics programmes are highly sequenced and report to be evidence-based. However, a Western Australian study found that even with the same programme, different educators obtained different results for their children (Louden, et al., 2005). It suggests that success probably depends less on the programme than on the instructor. If the programme resonates with the instructor, and they know why it works, then a commercially structured, systematic programme is a helpful adjunct to instruction.

Explicit systematic phonics instruction directs the child to phoneme-grapheme mapping to understand how the written language system works. Initially, there are only 26 letter-sound correspondences to master. The constrained number of 26 for alphabet knowledge, and initial letter-sound correspondences combined with the ability to manipulate them (decode and blend phonemes), consolidated in LTM, constitute the orthographic code: a H2H skill.

Once children understand and master this principle of direct mapping, they need to learn exceptions (e.g. /c/ followed by e, i, y changes the sound). English has 44 phonemes but only 26 graphemes so they will need to learn that group/s of graphemes can represent different phonemes (e.g. consonant digraphs such as /ch/ and vowel digraphs such as /ai/). According to the framework, this is the realm of H2G skills.

Figure 3 shows a schematic representation of the orthographic code and interacting elements. The relationships are not strictly hierarchical, but interactive and dynamic.

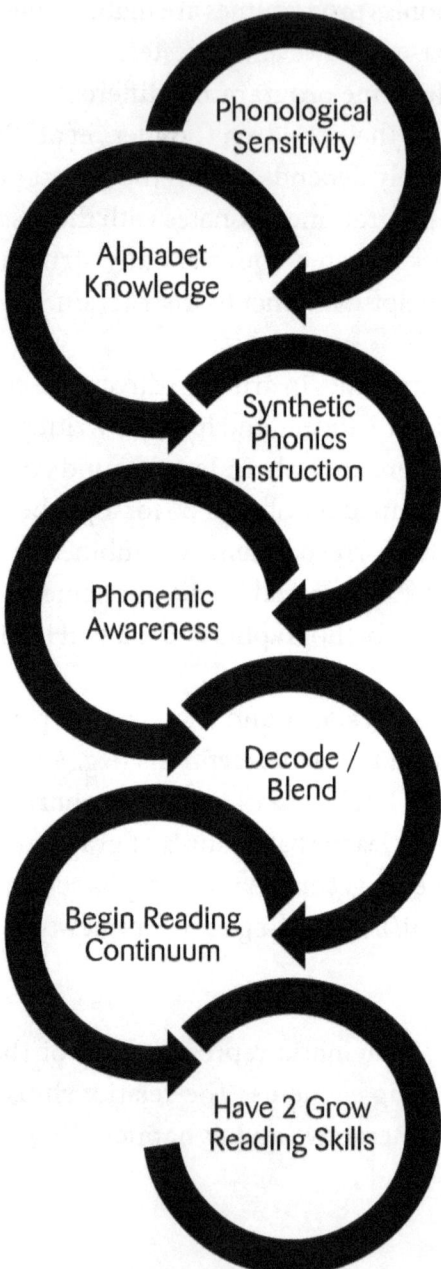

Figure 3. The interacting elements of the orthographic code

Constrained skills

I will now return to the notion of constrained skills because it has relevance to H2H skills.

Constrained skills show considerable variability during the period of acquisition. They are mastered by everyone eventually, whereas unconstrained skills retain variability over the life span (Paris, 2005). Constrained skills are phonemic awareness, acquiring the alphabetic principle and learning to handwrite the letters of the alphabet. Unconstrained skills are reading comprehension and written expression that continues to develop over a lifetime. In the period from around age four to seven years, most students come to understand written language. There is a transition from not reading to reading, demonstrating an ability to decode and blend phonemes; and from not writing to handwriting text, demonstrating an ability to independently retrieve and reproduce letterforms.

Paris (2005) argues this period shares four characteristics that limit our understanding of the developmental trajectory for reading and writing. The first characteristic is **unequal learning**. Some students learn to write letters but are unable to recite the alphabet correctly. Some know letter sounds but not letter names. When a cohort of students is 'learning' the alphabet, there is a lot of variation between students, but this is no longer the case under the second characteristic, which is **mastery**.

Skills develop from non-existent to fully acquired and so necessarily exhibit ceiling and floor effects for the so-called constrained skills. For example, the 26 letters of the alphabet represent a ceiling for learning. This period is relatively brief. Mastered skills appear to follow a similar pattern for many children. The initial acquisition of the skills is slow but then followed by a period of rapid learning that tapers off as mastery is achieved. It is important children are not discouraged before they hit the rise in their learning.

The third characteristic is **universality**. All competent readers know the same concepts of print, phonemic awareness, segment and blend in the same way. Compared to the similarity amongst readers over most of the life span, the differences during the acquisition of universally mastered skills (in terms of onset, rate or duration) are minor. Most students can learn to read and write with instruction by around seven years of age, although for some it costs more effort and requires individually targeted instruction. While much variability exists at school entry, in a relatively short time, similarity, in contrast to variability, between most students becomes evident.

The fourth characteristic is **co-dependency**. Letter name knowledge is a necessary, but insufficient skill, to read and write. The simultaneous and integrated development of language and literacy skills makes it difficult to separate relations between them during the acquisition phase. It is precisely for this reason that evaluation and analysis of literacy development, whilst it is acquired, is important. Performance variability is information that can assist educators to find the best fit, or zone of proximal development, for instruction. Once students can read and write, advanced skills for writing and reading becomes increasingly differentiated.

> *It simply is not true that there are hundreds*
> *of ways to learn to read [...]*
> *when it comes to reading we all have roughly the same*
> *brain that imposes the same constraints and the same*
> *learning sequence.*
> **Dehaene, 2009, p. 218**

In summary

This chapter presented a comprehensive description of the orthographic code as understood in the framework. The importance of alphabet knowledge was highlighted as integral to mastering the orthographic code. Phonics instruction is essential to build on this foundation, and to promote phonemic awareness. Phonemic awareness helps children to decode and blend sounds represented by letters in words and contributes to a conceptual understanding of the alphabetic principle.

The following chapter will discuss the graphomotor plan.

CHAPTER 6

The Graphomotor Plan

Learning to read improves when children are simultaneously taught how to write ... the research is very clear, you should teach writing at the same time as you teach reading. We need to absolutely still teach handwriting ... reading is not as good if you have not learnt to write the words.
Dehaene, 2019

Handwriting is a complex activity in which lower-level perceptual-motor (motor planning and execution) processes and higher-level cognitive (psycholinguistic and executive) processes continuously interact.
Graham & Weintraub, 1996

I recently enrolled in a course to learn Pitman shorthand. The instructor was very experienced having worked as a legal secretary for many years and enthusiastic about the system of shorthand and its origins. The forms devised by Pitman were based on curves of the circle, vertical, horizontal and diagonal lines. Unfortunately, the course was cancelled after one week due to lack of attendees, but before it was cancelled, I practised writing the strokes set as homework. It was difficult and frustrating. The same stroke could be written heavy or light depending on whether the sound it represented was voiced or not. How heavy, how light? Where to indicate the vowel sound? To the left or to the right? So many decisions!

Although I had invested some time in practising strokes I would never use, it did serve to prompt me to reflect on how a system of notation is devised and what it takes for others to learn it. First, the Pitman system used essentially the same strokes that all writing systems use – curves and lines in various configurations. Secondly, there were conventions for representing speech sounds: heavy or light strokes, placement of vowel sign to the right or left of the stroke, under the line or across the line. Thirdly, not only did I need to learn to write the strokes, I needed to be able to read them. Finally, shorthand was taught and practised by literate adults who have considerable tacit knowledge. The course had been scheduled for six weeks. But even in six weeks with some practise every day, I would have had to continue to write and read shorthand regularly thereafter to become proficient. It takes a long time to make cognitive changes that stick.

When it comes to English written language, just as the orthographic code needs to be cemented into cognitive architecture, so does the graphomotor plan. The graphomotor plan is here defined as a mental representation that combines what the letter 'looks' like with how to 'assemble' it as a motor plan. The motor plan is executed by hand and we evaluate the quality of the motor plan by handwriting performance. We can imagine the child initially assembling the motor plan stroke by stroke, but over time becoming more proficient as they get faster at retrieval of the letter representation and its assembly as a motor plan. Most children show rapid improvement in handwriting during Year 1 which reaches a plateau by Year 2 (Overvelde, 2013).

Handwriting is a special motor skill that distinguishes itself from most other motor skills in at least two ways. It needs to reproduce the shape of the letter in the absence of environmental spatial targets for the movement. The child must first have some mental representation of the spatial form of a letter to reproduce it. When they attempt to do this, the relationship between motor action and mental representation of the letter is strengthened because handwriting couples the visual and motor system (James & Engelhardt, 2012). Much weaker traces are left when children trace or type the letters.

When five- or six-year-old children are learning how to write the letters of the alphabet, they must acquire knowledge of the specific targets within each letter and the places where these targets have to be 'projected' onto paper. Most of this learning takes place in the conscious mode (Overvelde, 2013). During the learning process, children have to build up a representation of the letter form and movements necessary to produce the letter in cognitive architecture. Considerable variability is present when children are learning, followed by a large and rapid decrease in variability as performance improves. Variability becomes systematically smaller as practice continues. The graphomotor plan must be independently retrieved and reproduced according to convention. Learning to handwrite individual alphabet letters is a constrained skill that can be mastered by children by the end of Year 1.

However, some children may initiate active handwriting by free-form copying of a model letter before they enter school. Even so, it requires intense cognitive engagement and conscious control as the child endeavours to execute an accurate copy.

The following story of Sarah illustrates how effortful it is to learn to reproduce letterforms. Although Sarah's efforts occurred before formal instruction, it provides insight into how long it takes to build cognitive foundations for written language.

The story of Sarah

Sarah, a two-and-a-half-year-old child of college-educated parents was presented as a case study by McCarthy for how some children come to print by their name (McCarthy, 1977). Sarah became interested in learning to write after she had learnt the names of all letters in her name (SARH) from watching *Sesame Street* on television. Her parents had never taught her formally. Following the introduction of the letter Q, she asked an adult to draw the letter for her; she requested this several times before she attempted to do this herself. The first attempt was somewhat uneven. She handwrote hundreds of Qs before she realised the similarity with O. Sarah handwrote many notes and letters with a series of O, and Q in various combinations. A month later when making lines and circles she recognised she had made an A (it was half a circle with a line intersecting the middle).

Three months after recognising O, Sarah saw T on television and announced she could make that. Her handwriting lacked coordination and it was sometimes difficult for adults to read it, but Sarah consistently labelled it as T. Each time she displayed an interest in a letter, her parents demonstrated both upper and lower

The Graphomotor Plan

case until a preference was shown for one over the other. Upper-case letters dominated, but some such as 'i' may have been chosen as it was distinctive from their capital and the dot above the letter was always made with care. Other straight line letters followed L, H, F, E, followed by lines and loops B, P, R, D, followed by V, U. Letter formations demonstrated additional strokes and Sarah was three-and-a-half years old before she recognised diagonal lines in A and became able to handwrite correct letter formation. She began to confuse V and U at this stage. Because S was in her name, Sarah was highly motivated to handwrite it, but was unable to perceive how to start it and always began with a straight line before the curve.

At four years, she asked adults to 'start it', but she was unsuccessful in its execution. Very frustrated by her attempts, she stated she would never be able to write an S. Sarah was then given a sandpaper letter and encouraged to trace her finger along it as well as an S adult handwritten model. After ten tracings, she announced, 'I did it!'. Within a few weeks, she reverted to reversing the S. Repeated tracing helped for a few days, but then she reverted to reversal S. Although Sarah was highly motivated, this did not speed her acquisition to reproduce the S correctly, but there were some letters she was able to write independently. When adults would spell out words Sarah wanted to write, she had no difficulty with A, and D but needed help with Y.

Sarah learnt the letters of the alphabet in a distinctive pattern: circles (Q, O, A with curves); straight lines (L, H, i, E, F); lines and loops (B, R, P, D, m, n); and diagonal lines (K, W, X, M, N, A, V). The grouping of characteristics is thought to relate to the distinctive features, that is the contrastive features of the letters. Sarah would ask adults to show her how to write a letter and she would copy their handwritten form. If she was familiar with the letter, adults wrote the letter in lower and upper case in the air as well as on paper. As she became more familiar with the letter, she needed fewer clues. In the next stage, she used self-talk to help her to form the letters correctly. Sarah showed regressions in discriminating between letters with similar features when she was learning new letters and each new letter demanded immense concentration until the performance became routine.

McCarthy noted that Sarah never associated any sounds with the letters other than the letters in her name, suggesting she did not see the relationship between writing and reading. Sarah would 'read' her notes but the 'words' did not correspond with any of the written letters.

Sarah's acquisition of letters occurred in four stages according to McCarthy:
1. a letter model to be copied
2. more abstract means such as writing the named letter in the air, aided recall
3. consistent verbal cues to form letters (that became internalised)
4. letter names enabled her to reproduce its graphic form.

The probability is high, that Sarah would have gone on to be a competent reader with maturity and phonics instruction!

The developmental progression of Sarah's handwriting highlights the need for a model (environmental print), adult demonstration ('show me'), instruction about spatial targets ('to start it'), multisensory strategies (writing in the air, sandpaper letters) and cognitive strategies (self-talk and self-evaluation).

Principles for teaching handwriting

Irrespective of the writing system, written symbols are composed of a limited number of similar forms (Changizi, 2006). The conclusion is that these unique basic forms follow a universal distribution for all writing systems that closely parallels the features of natural scenes. It is not difficult to imagine tall tree trunks, the horizon, the moon in all its phases, hill inclines and descents and how these shapes could be reconfigured to form the conventional shape of alphabet letters. Visual recognition, rather than motor efficiency, is thought to be responsible for the forms adopted. Handwriting in English utilises a limited number of forms. Upper-case letters are big and little lines and big and little curves with limited spatial targets for starting the letter – at the top. Lowercase letters are essentially the same forms but have more complicated configurations, different spatial targets to start and terminate the letter, and overwriting of the same forms.

The first nine forms (|–O / \ + X ☐ △) of the Developmental Test of Visual Motor Integration (Beery, 1997), show a significant positive correlation with an ability to copy letterforms, but not beyond Year 1 (Marr & Cermak, 2002). This is because variations of the forms are used in our alphabet letters. However, it is not these nine forms that have meaning for written language, but the characteristic way the forms represent letters. Independent handwriting is not just about the graphomotor plan, it is also about the orthographic code. You need both to acquire written language.

To handwrite, children have to learn the distinct features of each letter and the conventions for their formation: where they start, the direction, orientation and sequence of the following strokes, and where strokes terminate. Children need explicit instruction about these spatial parameters, accompanied by demonstration and consistent verbal cues. The spatial sequence must be learnt by memorising and recalling the effective spatial targets that guide the writing movement (Overvelde, 2013). Frequent review aids independent retrieval.

The principles for handwriting instruction are frequent, explicit and systematic instruction with demonstration and modelling, (instructor) 'thinking aloud' during construction, and using consistent verbal cues. The letter name is used to introduce new letters. The name is thought to act as a memory aid to recall the mental representation of the letter from memory. Spatial targets and sequence of letter strokes are highlighted and adhered to. Children are encouraged to write the letter from memory, examine their efforts and make comparisons with the ideal model. Year 1 children benefit significantly from evaluating their work and setting small goals for themselves.

Commercial handwriting programmes
This book is agnostic about which handwriting font should be used to teach handwriting. Most schools use a manuscript font, but until recently cursive script (Victorian Modern Cursive) was required in Western Australian schools. The cursive script has additional entry and exit strokes to remember. The commercial handwriting books available for purchase by caregivers often rely upon tracing and copying. Neither is helpful without instructor monitoring, and neither is as effective as direct instruction. The crucial importance of spatial targets and sequencing of strokes for distinct letters has already been highlighted. Lack of monitoring at the learning stage leads to unhelpful motor habits that are very difficult to modify later. Children also become resistant to having to 'learn' another way of writing the letter. Instruct and monitor, irrespective of what programme is used. Tracing, in particular, requires less conscious effort so leaves weak neural traces for letter formation.

The Graphomotor Plan

Some programmes combine handwriting with phonics instruction. *Jolly Phonics* uses a sensory motor approach where children trace the letter with their fingers along rough tracks to give more tactile feedback. Letters are taught at the same time as the introduction of scheduled phonemes, for example, s-a-t-p-i-n.

Letterland has characters with alliterative names for its letters, for example, <f> is Firefighter Fred (up and over downward stroke for pole); <a> is Annie Apple (start with half-moon stroke to draw an apple). *Letterland* characters are coloured and some are obvious memory devices to associate with the letterform – Firefighter Fred has a red firefighter jacket, and Annie Apple is green.

Other programmes concentrate solely on handwriting. Western Australian educator Peggy Lego devised a handwriting programme based on seven shapes that she called movement patterns, which are slight variations on the first nine shapes of the Visual Motor Integration. Lego described her programme as 'an orally cued perceptual motor training programme ... to be controlled until the required action becomes habitual.' She was adamant that unsupervised tracing and copying contributed to 'the practice of error'. There are three phases to her approach:
- nursery rhymes and gross motor movements to introduce the oral-specific seven movement patterns
- fine motor development through the medium of art to reinforce oral-specific seven movement patterns
- use of oral-specific seven movement patterns to write letters and numbers.

Her movement patterns and verbal cues are still widely used in Western Australian schools. Letters are taught in order of their distinguishing features, for example, the verbal cue for <h> is tall man down, up over the gate. All children are encouraged to recite the verbal cue as they handwrite the letter (Lego, 1983).

Handwriting Without Tears (HWT) was developed by an American occupational therapist Jan Olsen, but it has international reach (Olsen, 1998). HWT is unique in that it emphasises learning to handwrite the upper-case letters first. Upper-case letters are introduced according to features, e.g. big curve letters, jump letters, M, N. Labels for spatial targets are explicitly taught such as top, bottom and middle. The student imitates the letter reciting the verbal cue as they are forming the letter. There is immediate correction by the instructor for letter formations incorrectly commenced or sequenced. Lower-case letters are introduced according to features. For example, the <c> is magic C and is responsible for a, c, g, o, q. Other letters are called 'diver letters', including h, m and n. All children are encouraged to recite the verbal cue as they handwrite the letter.

From this small selection, it should be obvious that there is not one programme that will resonate with all children. If there were, then there would be only one programme. Instead, educators might use a verbal cue that is particularly relevant in popular culture or they may tell a story to help remember the direction and/orientation of a troublesome letter. Children themselves make up stories to help them remember where to start, proceed and where to finish. What is important is that there is some consistency when introducing letters and monitoring formations so that instruction is explicit and systematic. Diverting from the script may be necessary, but usually only if the standard verbal cue does not resonate. Appendix 3 outlines a conservative timetable for handwriting instruction.

Figure 4 shows the universal shapes, lines and curves, used in both uppercase and lowercase letters. Some additional strokes may be necessary dependent upon font. For example, verbal cues for the entry stroke for Victorian Modern Cursive font may be 'start with a walking stick' or 'start with candy cane' and end 'with a small tick'.

Figure 4. Universal shapes for writing alphabet letters

The upper or lower case first?
Simone, working in Foundation Year, was heard complaining to her colleagues. 'Honestly, I don't know why these parents teach their kids to write their name. It's all in upper case. We have to start all over again and teach them properly.'

The debate about whether to teach upper or lower case first goes around and around. A study with over 400 children aged between three and five years found that most of the variation in handwriting abilities could be accounted for by age and whether or not they knew the name of the letter (Puranik, Petscher, & Lonigan, 2014). Younger children are more likely to write upper-case letters. From Drouin's study on the developmental progression of alphabet knowledge, we know that children recognise and name upper-case letters before lower-case letters. So, it might make intuitive sense to start with upper case. In France, children are taught upper-case letters in the first half of the Foundation Year and lower-case letters in the latter half of the year. However, others argue that reading books contain predominately lower-case letters, so it is better to start there. The EAK instruction protocol introduces the formation of both upper- and lower-case letters at the same time, but it is not a handwriting programme: its purpose is alphabet knowledge. What does not seem to be a good idea is to teach handwriting and practise both upper and lower case of the same letter, at the same time, when formal instruction is introduced (Thompson, 2009). For example, Aa, Bb, Cc and so on.

Similarly, there are debates about sensory-motor versus cognitive approaches for teaching handwriting. The evidence suggests that multisensory approaches are helpful in the beginning phase of handwriting instruction, but that cognitive approaches are more effective thereafter (Zwicker & Hadwin, 2009). Consolidating a graphomotor plan for letters requires cognitive engagement, attention, motivation and self-evaluation. The use of dotted thirds paper in Year 1 is a cognitive approach because the child must give additional attention to the limited space available to accommodate the letter's spatial parameters.

How to assess for independent recall
Learning to handwrite individual alphabet letters, in the absence of writing connected text, is a H2H constrained skill that can be mastered by children by the end of Year 1. The graphomotor plan must be independently retrieved and reproduced according to convention. The means to assess independent recall and reproduction of lower-case letters within a specified time limit has been assigned various labels in research studies: letter writing fluency, automaticity, orthographic-motor integration, or the Alphabet Task (Berninger, 1997). The label Alphabet Task (AT) is adopted here.

A recent systematic review of the relationship between the AT and literacy ability in Foundation Year found a strong positive relationship for writing composition, letter name and sound knowledge (Ray, Dally, Rowlandson, Tam, & Lane, 2022). The AT was administered by dictation (random or in alphabetic sequence) for either 15 or 60 seconds. One limitation of the AT in Foundation

Year was the floor effect, which means some children were unable to reproduce any letters within the specified time limit. Therefore, the AT is highly discriminating between Foundation Year children. Children cannot reproduce letters, or they can, and when they can they are more able to write text and to demonstrate letter name and sound knowledge. Because the AT demonstrates a H2H skill and reaches ceiling effect relatively quickly (all letters are independently retrieved and reproduced) the relationship between the AT and literacy ability is strongest in the first two years of school.

In Year 1, the time limit for the AT is typically 60 seconds. A study I conducted during Term 2 of Year 1, found that of 170 children, only 14% were able to write out all 26 letters in lower case in one minute. The results were consistent with other studies that found the average number of letters Year 1 children wrote for AT was 16 letters in one minute. The purpose of the AT in the context of H2H is to evaluate if children have consolidated the graphomotor plans for the letters of the alphabet. A time limit of two minutes is more realistic in the first half of the year. All reports of AT I have encountered assess only lower-case letters, but a separate test for upper-case letters is warranted to ensure children have mastered both. Figure 5 illustrates the range of AT performance in the same Year 1 classroom at the end of Term 2. The vertical line indicates the 15 second mark.

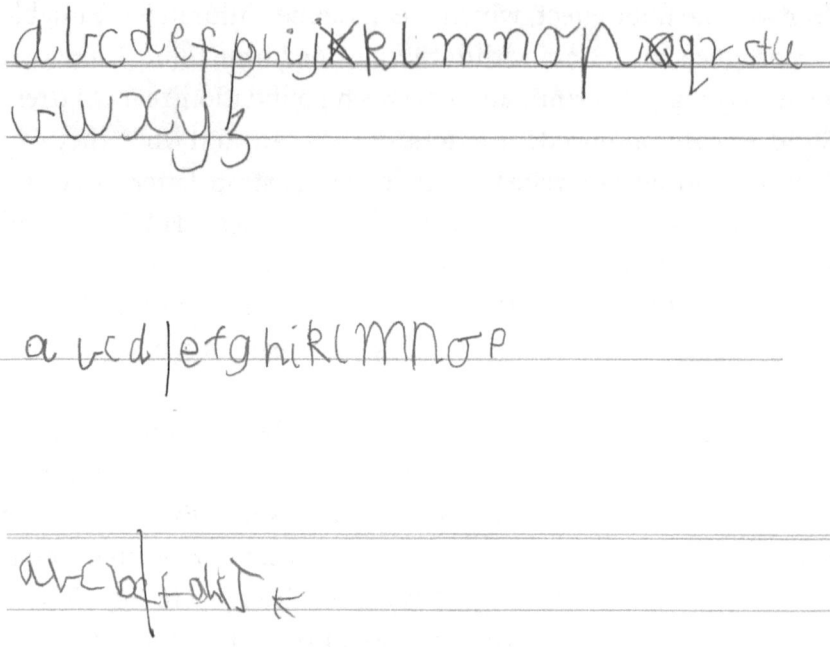

Figure 5. Range of responses to the Alphabet Task in Term 2: Year 1

The AT can be administered as a goal-free assessment, 'write out all the letters you know', to set a baseline at the beginning of Year 1 within a time limit set by the instructor. Educators use their judgement to quickly rank children's efforts; this is not time-consuming if you do not agonise over the ranking. Once ranked, typically three broad groups emerge: doing well, not sure, and not doing well. The children not doing well need additional support and further assessment sooner rather than later because consistent with the framework, they are also more likely to experience difficulty with the orthographic code. The not sure group are monitored because variability when learning to handwrite is not uncommon. As the year progresses, formative assessment (AT) can take place depending on the instruction schedule and educator's judgement.

The Graphomotor Plan

There is a strong positive correlation between the number of letters children recall in the AT and their ability to write a composition (Berninger, 1997).

Later in the year, children can be assessed for the graphomotor plan by the dictation of randomly ordered letters. Finally, children are assessed with the standard AT. The choice of paper is determined by the paper typically used in class for handwriting.

When administering the standard AT, the children are informed they will be writing out the lower-case letters of the alphabet, in order, across the page, in their best handwriting. Educators check for understanding of terms, the correct case, the right order, placement across the page and best handwriting. Demonstrating on the board may be helpful to reinforce what is required. Children are instructed to keep writing until the educator says STOP. If they finish before they hear STOP, then they can write out the alphabet again. As noted above, a time limit of two minutes is more realistic because the purpose is to assess for mastery in the first half of the year. Mastery is determined by the ability to independently recall a mental representation of alphabet letter/s, retrieve their graphomotor plan from memory and reproduce letter/s adhering to spatial parameters and sequencing of strokes according to convention for letterforms.

Figure 6 is a schematic representation of the demands for the graphomotor plan.

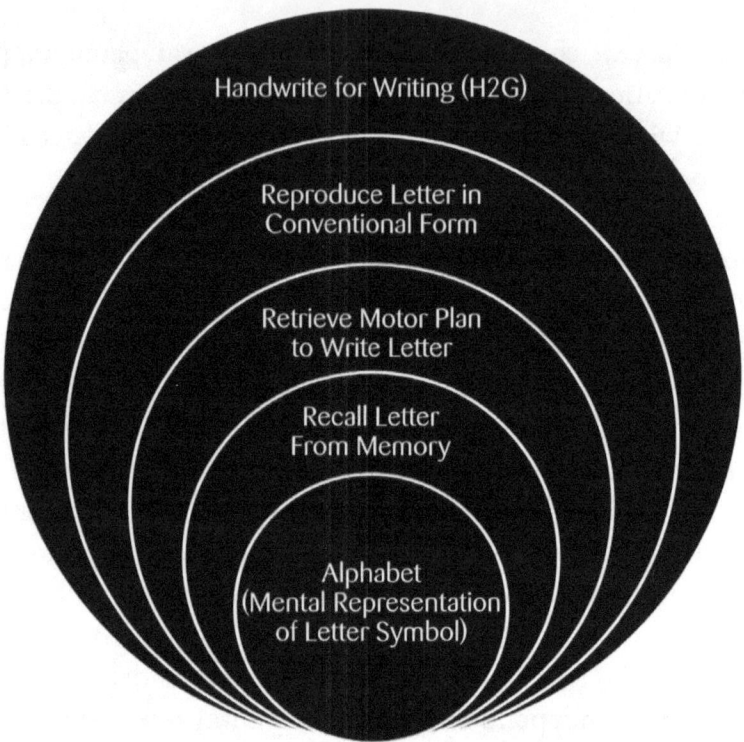

Figure 6. Schematic representation of graphomotor plan

In summary

This chapter presented a comprehensive definition of the graphomotor plan as understood in the framework. The importance of a mental representation of the letter in cognitive architecture (LTM), and the letter name as an aid to recall, was highlighted. To retrieve the graphomotor plan, explicit instruction and targeted practice is necessary to consolidate the plan in LTM. The quality of reproduced handwritten letters depends on adherence to characteristic features, and spatial parameters, of the letter. The Alphabet Task is a simple test is to assess for independent retrieval of the graphomotor plan. The following chapter revisits the idea of influences on written language acquisition.

CHAPTER 7

The Influences on Have to Have

A great change is coming over childhood in the world's richest countries. Today's rising generation is the first in which a majority are spending a large part of early childhood in some form of out-of-home child care.
Innocenti Report Card 8, 2008

The highest rate of return in early childhood development comes from investing as early as possible, from birth through age five, in disadvantaged families. Starting at age three or four is too little too late, as it fails to recognize that skills beget skills in a complementary and dynamic way. Efforts should focus on the first years for the greatest efficiency and effectiveness. The best investment is in quality early childhood development from birth to five for disadvantaged children and their families.
Statement for the Heckman Equation, 2012

Nothing happens in a vacuum; we are situated in time and place. As the first two chapters highlighted there are significant structural deficits in Australia that mean not all children have equal opportunities and/or outcomes in life. Not only are there environmental factors acting on the child from without, but also biological and genetic factors acting from within, which may influence the acquisition of written language. When influences make it easier to acquire written language, they are called Facilitator Influences (FI), but when they make it more difficult, they are called Detractor Influences (DI).

The environment

One way to understand the environment is to use Bronfenbrenner's ecological systems theory (Bronfenbrenner, 1986). It is visualised as a series of concentric circles around the individual child. Child development takes place in a complex system of relationships affected by multilevel environments. Those closest to the child are the home, school and the neighbourhood community. What happens there is influenced by changes in societal norms that influences, and is influenced by, the next level. At the local, state and federal government level there are policies and practice that drives, or is driven by, expectations of the adjunct levels. In turn, this, and/or all levels can be influenced by world events, such as war, natural disasters, and pandemics such as COVID.

> *There is good evidence that if people are disempowered if they have little control over their lives, if they are socially isolated or unable to participate fully in society, then there are biological effects.*
> **Michael Marmot**

Biology and genetics

Each of us is unique. We all have individual differences that make it easier or harder to live the life we are living. These individual differences interact with the environment, but even in highly supportive environments, some biological and/or genetic differences either make life more challenging or give us a leg up. Sometimes individual differences that are challenging in childhood become assets in adulthood, for example, sensitivity to taste and smell may lead to a career as a perfumer, chef or sommelier.

Facilitator influences

Sometimes FI are underappreciated because literacy develops as expected. It is not difficult to imagine an environment that acts as a FI. The child comes from a stable home with clear expectations and consistent routines. High-quality day or family care is available and nearby. There is no financial stress and caregivers spend time with the child in a print-rich environment; they have books at home, read to the child and visit the local library regularly. They speak English at home using a broad and varied vocabulary. The child is encouraged to ask questions, but also encouraged to sort out problems for themselves. The neighbourhood has cycling paths, shaded nature playgrounds, and there is a swimming pool nearby. The local government is keen to support the community and provides several venues for parent and club groups.

Similarly, biological and genetic factors facilitate literacy. In general, they are children described as neurotypical, in good health, and displaying appropriate school readiness skills. There is no identifiable vulnerability. They pay attention to instruction, like learning, work hard, and are willing to strive to achieve a goal.

The child has good friends and gets along well with adults and peers. They are amongst the oldest in their class cohort.

Detractor influences

In contrast, environments that act as DI are where there is financial stress, insecure housing, a chaotic home with little routine, trauma and several adverse family events. They may live in neighbourhoods of social disadvantage, with a lack of public transport, poor access to health facilities, and limited community facilities such as parks and libraries. The school may lack facilities and specialists to provide assessment and targeted intervention. Governments at all levels may act as DI by maintaining disadvantages through flawed policies.

In contrast to neurotypical, some children present as neurodiverse. They may present with developmental differences which mean acquiring literacy is more challenging. Sometimes children are diagnosed with developmental disorders such as autism spectrum disorder (ASD), attention deficit hyperactivity disorder (ADHD), developmental coordination disorder (DCD), sensory processing disorder (SPD) or they may have sensory impairments such as hearing or visual challenges. Dyslexia may be a familial trait. Most developmental challenges are comorbid, which means they often overlap in presentation, for example, a child may have challenges with attention, but also with motor performance.

Other external factors that can impact learning include medical conditions that affect school attendance, or being amongst the youngest in the class cohort and therefore possessing less maturity to attend and focus.

In summary

This chapter presented an overview of the influences that make it easier or more difficult to acquire written language. It is for this reason that they are important to consider when progress is not as expected. There are many creative ways educators can mitigate the effect of DI and enhance the effects of FI every day in their interactions with children. While the advocacy role is not explored in this book, it is worth reflecting on how we can best influence policy to support children with whom we come in contact.

The following chapter discusses in more detail the facilitatory and detractor nature of the environmental influence.

CHAPTER 8

The Environment in Which I Live

It has been said that it takes a village to raise a child. Today, the local village is hard to find.

The family into which a child is born plays a powerful role in determining lifetime opportunities. This is hardly news, but it bears repeating: some kids win the lottery at birth, far too many don't – and most people have a hard time catching up over the rest of their lives. Children raised in disadvantaged environments are not only much less likely to succeed in school or society, but they are also much less likely to be healthy adults. A variety of studies show that factors determined before the end of high school contribute to roughly half of lifetime earnings inequality. This is where our blind spot lies: success nominally attributed to the beneficial effects of education, especially graduating from college, is in truth largely a result of factors determined long before children even enter school.
Heckman, from 'Lifelines for Poor Children', The New York Times, 15 September 2013

In 1970, a book called *Future Shock* (Toffler, 1970) was published. It went on to be a New York Times bestseller. The thesis of the book was that the world has always been changing, but now it appears to do so at a faster rate. This appears prescient half a century later. We live in a global world of rapidly emerging technologies, are flooded with information and are often left feeling overwhelmed – and there's no doubt that our children often feel this way too.

Nestled in a complex society with many competing voices, there is pressure on politicians, educators, parents and children. Conflicting opinions about how children learn, how they should behave, what should be the focus of attention, the use of screen time and technology in general, are all up for debate. Amid contested opinions, we are often seduced into grabbing onto what is promised as the magic bullet because it is too difficult to sort through it all.

There is no magic bullet to learning to read and write. It is hard work to acquire the H2H skills, the orthographic code and graphomotor plan. Some children come to school reading and handwriting but most learn to do so during the first two years at school. Failure in the early years can have a devastating effect on children that may negatively influence their future lives. The impact of the environment can either act as a FI to facilitate written language acquisition or as a DI to detract from written language acquisition.

Facilitator influence – environment

Home
Children born into families of social and economic advantage are more likely to live in homes that are print rich. Environments that act as FI have stable caregivers, regular routines for sleep and mealtimes, and the children are positively involved with siblings

and their loving extended family. Children in a FI environment meet their milestones for motor, language, social, emotional and play development, and are less likely to display developmental vulnerabilities at school entry.

There is minimal evidence that parents can teach children to read simply by reading to them (Senechal, LeFevre, Thomas, & Daley, 1998) and most children do not acquire written language without explicit instruction. However, reading to children is important for literacy development as a shared experience and exposure to oral language. In addition, one study of home practices found that drawing preschool children's attention to print around them built stronger foundations for later literacy development (Phillips, Norris, & Anderson, 2008).

Some examples of home practices include:
- matching letters
- identifying letter names and letter sounds
- listening to, and playing with, sounds that rhyme
- analysing word meanings together
- identifying colours and colour words
- teaching children to write and spell their name
- helping children to make explicit connections between the stories they heard and their background knowledge.

Daycare
Many aspects of quality out-of-home provision are environmental correlates of beneficial home literacy practices as outlined above. Children appear to do well in institutional environments that actively support their development through play. Caregivers are responsive and conversations with children are contingent upon the children's activities.

The Effective Provision of Preschool Education (EPPE) study conducted in the UK applied environmental rating scales to identify quality educational provision in several settings for children from the age of three: nursery daycare, play groups, private daycare, nursery schools and local authority daycare (Sylva, Melhuish, Sammons, Saraj-Blatchford, & Taggart, 2004).

The characteristics that qualified as quality indicators were:
- staff used open-ended questions and encouraged 'sustained shared thinking'
- differentiated learning opportunities were provided
- a balance between staff-supported freely chosen play and staff-led small group activities
- the staff viewed educational and social development as complementary
- staff were well trained and had a good understanding of appropriate pedagogical content
- staff supported children being assertive at the same time encouraging social problem-solving
- there was strong leadership (the manager of the facility was a trained educator) with small staff turnover
- there was strong parental involvement and parents shared the educational aims of the facility for their children.

School
Not all children enter school with the same literacy skills related to reading and writing. The need for a developmental understanding of literacy instruction has been highlighted.

The potency of developmentally informed instruction was demonstrated in a USA study, which conducted naturalistic observations of language instruction in four Grade 1 classrooms (Juel, 1988). Considerable variation in instructional practice was found between them. Each classroom had no more than 17 students and classrooms divided students into three reading groups that reflected their literacy skills.

Classroom 1 was labelled traditional, in the main because students received the same instruction regardless of their literacy levels.

Classroom 2 provided differentiated instruction with middle and low groups involved in word sorts. The low group also received teacher modelling on how to chunk words, mainly restricted to onset-rime.

Classroom 3 made extensive use of trade books and all the reading groups spent time writing in their journals. There was little direct phonics instruction and the teacher relied on peer coaching to facilitate word recognition.

Classroom 4 was the most phonics-orientated and instruction differed considerably between groups. Instruction also changed as the year progressed. By mid-year, the highly sequenced phonics curriculum conducted with the low group was completed. Instruction changed to involve more discussion of vocabulary and text.

No pre-test differences for the low reading group in each classroom had been detected. In a post-test by the end of the year, all children in the low group in Classroom 4 were reading at or near grade level. Children with high literacy skills at school entry did better in Classroom 3 with less phonics and more time spent reading and writing. However, the most successful classroom overall was Classroom 4 because all the students could read by the end of the year. Classroom 4 provided differentiated, structured and sequential instruction mapped to the results of literacy assessment at school entry.

Research into teacher practice in Australia also adopted naturalistic observations in classrooms all over Australia. The study, *In Teachers Hands*, was conducted nationwide with Year 1 and Year 2 children and teachers (Louden, et al., 2005). The aim was to report teaching practices that improved literacy outcomes.

Teacher literacy practices were assessed across six domains: participation, knowledge, orchestration, support, differentiation and respect. The criterion of teacher effectiveness was assigned based on children's assessment achievement before the conducted observations. Multilevel analysis was used to determine effective teaching practice, which was based on children's prior performance and observation of teacher classroom practice. Effective teachers enabled their children to perform significantly above expected levels for their class grade. The study found no difference in generic literacy activities in the early years (phonics, shared book reading, modelled writing) between effective and less effective teachers. However, effective teachers demonstrated a wider range of literacy practices than less effective teachers did. Effective teachers taught phonics within a wider context of reading, writing and spelling lessons, and focused on text-level features. In addition, effective teachers possessed extensive literacy teaching repertoires that enabled them to adjust pace, adopt metalanguage to extend concepts, extend feedback and provide challenges according to classroom ability levels. It is salient that the same activities were used by both effective and less effective teachers, yet with the same activities effective teachers educated their children to achieve significantly above grade level expectations for literacy.

Early differentiated instruction resonates with the third characteristic nominated by Paris, that of **universality**. Children demonstrate considerable variability in literacy development when they enter school. Nevertheless, effective teachers expect their children to learn to read and write and they understand their role as educators is to narrow the distribution of constrained skills. A goal of an effective educator is the child's mastery of constrained skills. Effective educators reduce inter-child variability during the acquisition of universally mastered skills (Paris, 2005).

Easy to access specialist literacy support for both children and junior educators, and easy access to allied health specialists for consultation and direct service provision act as facilitator influences.

Detractor influence – environment

Government policy and practice

There are numerous DI in Australia related to postcodes – rural and remote areas in Australia, the concentration of socioeconomic disadvantage in regional towns and lack of employment opportunities for provider caregivers, to name but a few. Housing stress, overcrowding, concern for safety and high crime convictions may also disrupt community cohesion (Drane, 2020). Chaotic households do less well to support children's attention and completion of required tasks. Insufficient or poor nutrition can contribute to dental, physical and mental health problems.

> *Early childhood programs should be evaluated using a full range of skills that enable children to become more productive adults. Many analysts equate program effectiveness with performance on short-term measures of cognition that poorly predict life success. Socioemotional skills – such as attentiveness, impulse control, sociability and conscientiousness – are primary*

> *drivers of achievement, health, and increased social and economic productivity. Unfortunately, these skills often go unmeasured.*
> **Heckman from 'Early childhood education and social mobility', Vox EU, 12 January 2016**

At the local government level, there may be a lack of library facilities, interesting and challenging playgrounds and adequate parent-child supports such as childcare or preschool facilities. This is important because studies with school-age children show a positive relationship between cognition and motor performance (Piek, Dawson, Smith, & Gasson, 2008). Indeed, activities such as jumping, running, marching, hopping, climbing, cycling, clapping and dancing, reinforce rhythmic patterns reminiscent of alternating stress patterns in syllabic structures found in English phonology. Physical activity is positively correlated with daily living abilities, sleep and paying attention.

The Early Development Index (later AEDI), a marker for school readiness, found a strong negative correlation between letter-identification tasks and the EDI domain Physical Health and Wellbeing (Keating, 2007). Although this finding was queried, the contribution of sensory-motor development to written language cannot be underestimated, particularly when children in industrialised societies appear to have less opportunity or less motivation to physically engage with the environment around them. Directional language related to letter formations is first experienced and understood by children in their bodies, in the sense of embodied cognition (e.g. up, down, around, small, big, across).

At the community level, some children experience adverse childhood events associated with abuse, neglect and household challenges. Trauma has a deleterious effect on children's learning.

Hypervigilance, as a result of trauma, negatively affects focus and attention. Transition periods to acquire written language may be longer than for children who have not experienced trauma and neglect.

Society expectations
Societal habits change over time, which dynamically impacts the relationship between motor and cognitive development. For example, parents were advised to place their babies on their backs (supine) when they sleep to prevent infant death syndrome. But early studies showed delays in gross motor development of typical babies at six months when this practice became widespread (Dewey, Fleming, & Golding, 1998). So now the advice is to place babies in the prone position, tummy time, when awake to counteract the deleterious effects of supine sleeping.

The long-term effects for posture, core stability and aerobic fitness due to reduced movement experiences such as less tummy time, limited physical activity due to smaller residential outdoor play areas and safety concerns, increased sedentary screen time, and more time spent in vehicle transit, are hard to quantify. These societal changes may subtly exacerbate developmental vulnerability related to motor coordination, attention and listening, processing and integrating internal and external sensory information.

Fine motor activities such as colouring, cutting and pasting, occur in every preschool setting and build strong cognitive foundations for later literacy instruction. But the positive effects of daily opportunities to engage with everyday practical materials at home to promote fine motor abilities should not be underestimated. The domestic life that children occupy today is different to that of 50 years ago when engaging in simple household tasks was more commonplace. Multiple occasions to sweep the veranda, shovel in the garden, water the pot plants, squeeze the sponge to wipe the table, fold flannels and tea towels, stir the cake mix, peel potatoes, to name a few, have become less accessible as domestic arrangements have changed.

Social contributors to the detractor effects of the environment

Over-reliance on online learning
Since the introduction of the World Wide Web (www) in 2008, there has been an over-reliance on computer technology in place of face-to-face instruction. This starts early. Children are given electronic toys to sing the alphabet or tablets to 'learn' to handwrite. Magical powers assigned to computer technology and online education in particular showed that it did not live up to the hype during the natural experiment of COVID. Even committed adults find it difficult to maintain online education as the history of Massive Open Online Courses (MOOC) demonstrates; and, in the beginning, most of those quality courses were free. There is a difference between using screen technology as an adjunct to learning versus being the primary means of instruction. The *Sesame Street* experiment is salient in this regard.

Educators are devalued
With each educational review, there are calls for more accountability and the need for more testing. Constant berating and reduction in status have led to experienced educators leaving the profession, which compounds the problem. The expertise of the educator has a big impact on the child's learning, although learning always involves at least two things: the motivation, talents and backgrounds of the teacher, and those of the child (Hattie & Zierer, 2019).

Poor school attendance

The children with the most needs may not be attending school. In some cases, the sensitivity of the child's background makes this a difficult problem to address with current resources. Some schools have become very creative to reduce barriers such as breakfast clubs, providing uniforms, and paying for excursions. However, school budget constraints and community disengagement may remain limiting factors.

Medical conditions may interfere with school attendance and is potentially a serious dilemma for the child, caregiver and the school. Agencies such as schools in the hospital, distance education services, and/or homeschooling are options but they need to be available and accessible. Unfortunately, this is not always the case.

Today, school refusal is on the increase, which may be a response to COVID lockdowns. The longer children refuse to go to school, the more difficult it is to rejoin their peers. School refusal may be due to children feeling inadequate in their ability to keep up compared to their peers. In that case, reframing the child's current performance using the framework might help to identify where it is breaking down, to provide targeted intervention.

Increase in working parents and childcare

The disadvantage of multiple caregivers, which need not be detrimental, is the possible loss of contingent learning. Multiple caregivers may find it more challenging to build on what the child already knows. All children need consistent and responsive caregivers, but some need it more than most.

> *There are large gaps in skills and development at the point of entry to school: many more low SES children are behind compared to their high SES peers. The gaps exist across*

all domains, across all skill areas, and are even larger at later stages of school and into adulthood. The results are consistent with research that has repeatedly demonstrated that social background is a key predictor of educational and future success. Moreover, the performance gaps by social class manifest in the earliest years of children's lives and fail to narrow in the years that follow, such that children who start behind often stay behind.
Education Opportunities, 2020

In summary

This chapter presented an overview of environmental influences that facilitate or detract from written language acquisition. While some are beyond our control, we can promote activities that support building foundations for written language. For example, we may need to rethink safety versus risk (use of playground equipment and gross motor play), contributing to household chores versus accepting a less-than-perfect job, walking or cycling instead of taking the car. Every opportunity denied is an opportunity lost to build strong foundations for literacy development. The way we live our lives today makes it generally more difficult to provide consistency, community and control over exposure to world events for our children. We need to be cognisant of what is at stake and reflect upon what it means for the academic progress of children.

The following chapter discusses in more detail the facilitatory and detractor nature of the biological and genetic influence.

CHAPTER 9

The Body & Brain I Inhabit

...the first two years of life are a crucial period for the development of strategies for regulating negative emotions, coping with frustrations and maintaining psychological equilibrium.
Lewis et al., 2004

... the most common diagnoses or associated conditions in the children treated with handwriting difficulties by occupational therapists were learning difficulties (including ADHD), coordination difficulties (including developmental coordination disorder), and autism spectrum disorders.
Brossard-Racine, 2012

Stephen was a bright boy but struggled to learn to read and write. By the time he was diagnosed with dyslexia in Year 3, Stephen was ready to embrace his diagnosis. He was not stupid, instead he had dyslexia. He did a presentation for his class about dyslexia, how it had affected him when he started school, and how he was learning to address it in his life. It was no longer a secret why he was slow to read and write – it was his dyslexia and Stephen was working to beat it.

The previous chapter dealt with external influences but there are also internal influences that either facilitate or detract from acquiring written language. Biology can be defined as our individual constitutional makeup: these can relate to sensory processing, motor coordination, executive functioning, working memory capacity and processing speeds to name a few. These are correlated, either positively or negatively, with learning to read and write.

Dyslexia is a genetically-based condition, but not dependent on a single gene so its presentation can be different for different children. Dyslexia is recognised as having more difficulty acquiring H2H skills and is considered a problem with the conversion of written symbols into speech sounds. When children with dyslexia learn the bidirectional relationship between graphemes and phonemes, their phonemic awareness improves and consolidates the alphabetic principle (Shaywitz, 2020).

The term neurodiversity is used to describe a range of developmental differences that manifest as challenges in managing everyday activities, including learning. Developmental differences are generally not confined to one manifestation, rather they are comorbid with one or more other developmental differences. For example, a child with attention difficulties may also have motor coordination challenges, at the same time experiencing more sensory sensitivity to touch and noise than their peers. However, neurodiversity does not mean children cannot learn. They certainly can and many excel. Indeed, it is important to identify the strengths of children with neurodiverse needs. Neurodiversity includes challenges with motor coordination, attention and focus, self-regulation, social interaction, sensory processing differences, mental health, and facility with language. It may be better to describe these differences by the term developmental vulnerability until children receive a diagnosis. It is important to understand neurotypical children may also have extended transition periods for acquiring written language, for example, being the youngest in age compared to the class cohort.

Facilitator influences make it easier to acquire written language and detractor influences make it more challenging. Where DI makes learning more challenging, children may need more time with explicit, systematic instruction; or instruction is modified according to the task.

Internal facilitator influences

Just as there are environmental facilitators, so there are body and brain facilitators that can be viewed as contributions by the child to the acquisition of written language. In most English-speaking countries, typically developing children are thought to be ready to benefit from formal handwriting instruction in the latter half of the Foundation Year. But optimal support for children's readiness to achieve a graphomotor plan for letter/s, requires the integrity of a number of sensorimotor systems: motor, sensory and perceptual systems.

Sensory motor development
The contribution of sensory motor development to cognition and how we understand the world is significant. Sensory information through our senses – sight, sound, touch, taste, smell, proprioception and vestibular sensation – modifies our motor responses. Typical sensory processing results in an adaptive motor response being generated. But if children experience inefficient or inadequate sensory information from their sensory systems, then they may have less than optimal motor responses. For example, some children find the noise in an open plan classroom 'too much' to be able to block noise out and attend to instruction. Or, some children need more proprioceptive feedback to determine the amount of force necessary to hold or move things (e.g. pressing down too hard with pencil on paper).

The proprioception and vestibular sensory systems impact the grading of movement, balance and responses to gravity, which influence children's core strength, posture and bilateral coordination. The vestibular system provides information about movement, gravity and changing head positions. It tells us whether we are moving or remaining still, as well as, the direction and speed of movement. It relates to the visual system and helps us to maintain a stable visual field. It also relates to the auditory system as both respond to vibration (e.g. music and dance an obvious example), and helps us know where we are in space. Proprioception is the unconscious awareness of body position, and helps create a 'body map'. It tells us about the position of our body parts, their relations to each and their relation to other people and objects.

Integration of sensory, motor and perceptual systems supports bilateral coordination so that children are able to cross the midline and use both sides of their body cooperatively. Bilateral coordination is necessary to complete many self-care tasks, to stabilise the paper when drawing, and to manipulate objects.

Everyday play enables children to explore objects and their properties. Recognising texture, weight and temperature as well as geometric properties such as size and shape, supports fine motor development. Hands-on means of cognitively engaging with letters are multisensory approaches to introduce letters and numbers in the home or daycare, for example, 3D letter representations found in wooden puzzles, letters/numbers on the fridge, sandpaper and play doh letters. The positive relationship between sensation and cognition was demonstrated by kindergarten children who were encouraged to touch and explore 3D letters and numbers. Touching and feeling to recognise a letter is known as haptic perception. When these children were compared to a control group, they did better at decoding pseudowords. Handling the letters appeared to facilitate a mental representation of the letter. Haptic exploration (touch) facilitates the dynamic relationship between the orthographic and phonological representation of the letter because children must process it more analytically (Bara & Gentaz, 2011).

Fine motor development coupled with cognitive maturity promotes children's tool use. The ability to use writing tools enables children to demonstrate a number of graphic behaviours associated with handwriting.

Drawings and shapes
A positive relationship exists between children's ability to draw and learning to handwrite. There are two discernible conceptual progressions in children's graphic behaviours. First, they engage in graphic behaviours intentionally. Secondly, they start to attach meaning to their drawings. In one study preschool children aged between three to four years were presented with two tasks to examine the correlation between drawing and handwriting. In the first task, children were presented with an **object** (toy horse, dog, cow, doll, car) that was then placed in a box with a lid to remove

it from view. The children were instructed to put 'something on paper' to help them remember the object. In the second task, they were presented with a **picture** of the same object that was placed in an envelope to remove it from view. As before, the children were instructed to 'put something on paper' to help them remember the picture. The younger children tended to make undifferentiated markings for the object or picture and did not make any letters in their drawings. Older children tended to make representational drawings and letter-like shapes to depict what was in the box or envelope. The same children were tested again in Grade 1. Children who made representational drawings and letter/letter-like shapes in the previous test performed significantly better at handwritten literacy tasks than those who had used simple tags to depict the objects (Martlew & Sorsby, 1994), demonstrating a positive correlation between drawing ability and handwriting.

Name writing
Writing one's name is usually the first stable written letter sequence that children achieve and early attempts are usually in uppercase letters (Treiman & Kessler, 2004). Children who grow up in print-rich environments become interested in print when they recognise their names or letters in their names. Remember the story of Sarah. The length of a child's name does not appear to afford an advantage or disadvantage when literacy measures are compared; rather, it is the proficiency for writing one's name, not the length of the name that appears to represent a threshold for written language (Puranik & Lonigan, 2012).

The contribution of graphic behaviours to written language appears to converge around the age of four to seven years to enable children to distinguish specific forms that have a specific meaning. It ignites the child's interest to reproduce these forms in specific ways to communicate. Graphic behaviours are positively related to handwriting when there is a transition to representational drawings and name writing.

Pencil grasp

Pencil grasp makes an obvious contribution to handwriting. The recommended pencil grasp for handwriting, dynamic tripod, is rarely present before four years of age. Before four years of age, a developmental progression of at least five grasps has been identified (Schneck, 1990). From the age of four to seven years, the range from transitional to mature grasp is apparent, the most common being dynamic tripod and/or lateral tripod grasp. The pencil grasp may show increased variability during this transition phase before children settle into a mature grasp. Different pencil grasp trajectories for drawing or colouring were noted in typically developing children aged from three to seven years that reflected the discrete intrinsic hand muscle activity necessary for different tasks. This specificity suggests children's prehensile engagement with their environment before school needs to be broad and varied. Children presented with increased opportunities to practise using their hands in a wide variety of activities in actively supportive environments improve fine motor abilities; these children are more likely to develop a dynamic tripod grasp for handwriting.

Internal possible detractor influences

Visual perceptual skills

In order to read, visual acuity is important and corrective lens may be necessary, but interpretation of a visual stimulus involves cognition. Visual-cognitive components include visual attention, visual memory and visual discrimination, which support visual-motor integration to handwrite.

Continued reversals, apparent inability to discriminate between upper- and lower-case letters or different font of the same letter, incomplete letter formations, and poor line placement have all been attributed to visual perceptual difficulties. How visual perception contributes to handwriting is not precisely determined, but weak visual perceptual skills correlate with weak handwriting skills when children are learning to handwrite (Feder & Majnemer, 2007). Often, weak visual perceptual skills are comorbid with other developmental vulnerabilities that detract from acquiring the H2H skills.

General strategies to support visual perception could be:
- Reduce visual clutter
- Draw attention to discriminating features
- Multisensory approach when introducing letters
- Use of different colours for vowels to distinguish from consonants
- Use of vertical surfaces to draw and write (outdoor blackboards/whiteboards)
- *Where's Wally* or equivalent to encourage scanning and figure-ground discrimination
- Alert children to different fonts and case of letter/s and that it remains representative of the same sound despite different appearance
- Spend time outdoors scanning and locating landmarks.

Attention
Attention plays a key role in the acquisition of written language. Children must visually attend to letters, listen to distinguish between contrastive sounds, and accurately reproduce letters according to their characteristic features. An early study showed that easily distracted kindergarten children were more likely to produce form errors when copying letters (Simner, 1986). Form errors took place more often during the final stages of writing the letter than during

the initial stage of letter construction. It suggests that where to start the letter stroke, sequence and follow through, and where to terminate the letter, should be reinforced during instruction, especially for children with attention difficulties.

Neuroimaging studies support the role of conscious attention (prefrontal cortex) especially during the acquisition phase of written language. (Palmis, et al., 2021).

Oral language
The contribution of oral language to early written language seems intuitive but oral language is not highly correlated with learning to read; however, oral language is positively correlated with reading comprehension (Shanahan, 2006). Oral language is not only about vocabulary, but rather a reflection of cognitive architecture for language such as syntax, semantics and how to use language in social situations (pragmatics). Children from environments where caregivers help children extend their communication through circles of questions and answers contingent upon each other do better at oral language. Extended circles of communication are a necessary skill to solve everyday social problems, such as obtaining a desired toy or requesting a drink. Oral language plays a role in memory retrieval and therefore supports memory structures.

An Australian longitudinal study investigated patterns and predictors of children's oral language and literacy abilities at four, six, eight and ten years. The findings challenged the common view that children's progress along the oral-to-literate continuum is stable and predictable.

The following developmental patterns emerged (Zubrick, Taylor, & Christianson, 2015):
- children started with low oral language performance at four years that remained so at ten years

- children started with low oral language at four years but consistently improved
- children started with low oral language at four, but improved at eight, then declined at ten years
- children started with high oral language at four and retained high oral language at ten years
- children started with high oral language at four but declined at ten years
- children showed a fluctuating pattern at each of the year levels.

The following chapter presents a dynamic systems perspective for children's development and may provide some food for thought regarding these counterintuitive findings.

Common challenges
A common challenge associated with diagnosed developmental vulnerability is smaller capacity working memory (WM) and slower processing speeds (Gathercole & Alloway, 2008). However, many so-called neurotypical people also exhibit this individual difference. A small capacity WM means that children need exposure, time, monitored practice and feedback to commit knowledge to long-term memory (LTM). It does not mean they cannot learn. If knowledge is poorly consolidated in LTM, then recall and retrieval becomes difficult.

Children who have a diagnosis of attention disorders, often have more difficulty with verbal WM (Capodieci, 2018). In Foundation Year, they benefit from multisensory approaches to handle letters, write in sand, and make playdoh letters, in addition to verbal instruction. By Year 1 these stronger mental representations of letters will facilitate paying attention to their crucial spatial parameters.

Children who have a diagnosis of autism spectrum disorder, often benefit from additional visual cues (Handle, 2022). They may need a dot on the page to indicate where to start, and an arrow to indicate the direction of the strokes to learn letter graphomotor plans. Tracing letters using this method can be useful in the beginning, but such accommodations during the acquisition phase should be quickly withdrawn as the child becomes more confident in knowing where to start and how to proceed.

Children who have a diagnosis of motor coordination disorder, benefit from explicit systematic instruction, monitoring and feedback to support motor learning, with particular attention to spatial parameters. Three different approaches to support attention to size and placement are:
- dotted thirds using sky, grass and ground analogy – sky for upper-case and ascender letters and ground for descender letters
- dotted thirds using the cat or seahorse analogy – cat's head for uppercase and ascender letters, cat's body for body letters, and cat's tail for descender letters
- differentiating size e.g. Size 1 are for upper-case and ascender letters, Size 2 for body letters and Size 3 for descender letters (dotted thirds make this easier to apply).

Different approaches appeal to different children, so if one does not work ask the child which one would help them to remember and be consistent thereafter with verbal cues.

Highly anxious children may be reluctant to reproduce a letterform they believe will be imperfect. Instructor demonstration with consistent verbal cues will help. They may benefit from tracing with an arrow cue in the beginning. However, they still require adult monitoring as they form the letter. Give immediate feedback and withdraw tracing to avoid dependence, and instead encourage copying a model letter, and then to handwrite the letter from memory.

Children who have a family history of dyslexia, respond well to explicit, systematic instruction and can acquire the H2H skills as other children, although it may take longer to do so and they may have to work harder to achieve fluency. Depending on the child, they may benefit from additional strategies such as multisensory approaches and/or visual cues when learning to handwrite.

Beyond the Have to Have stage
This book is about the acquisition of written language, so the expectation is that children will learn to handwrite the letters of the alphabet, retrieve them from memory and reproduce them according to conventional forms. However, challenges with H2G skills are likely when children have smaller WM capacity and slower processing speeds. This is all the more reason to master the H2H skills. Reading comprehension and composition make big demands on WM. Robust structures in LTM mitigate the limitations of a smaller-capacity WM.

In summary

This chapter presented an overview of the biological/genetic influences that facilitate or detract from written language acquisition. Advances in education, health and neuroscience mean that some detractor influences can be mitigated. But we cannot be complacent when things are going well. Studies have shown that children may begin on track but then lose their way. Small changes in children's circumstances can have a big effect on their progress.

The following chapter introduces a dynamic system perspective as a way to understand this phenomenon.

CHAPTER 10

The Dynamic System Perspective

The elementary school years are characterised by dramatic advancements in some areas, gradual evolving capabilities in others, and plateaus or even declines in development.
Graham & Weintraub, 1996

Deficit approaches to learning tend to focus on the things that children cannot do; the outcome is a 'fix-it' approach. In contrast, developmental models build on and scaffold the existing knowledge bases of every student.
Griffin et.al., 2007

We are all inclined toward one belief system or another when it comes to child development. I lean toward a dynamic system perspective (DSP) because it helps me make sense of the transition period from school entry to Year 2 entry.

In the mid-20th century two child development theories significantly influenced literacy pedagogy: the cognitivist or developmental constructivism approach (Piaget) and the sociocultural or social constructivism approach (Vygotsky). Although both Piaget and Vygotsky emphasised language (oral speech, gesture and inner speech or self-talk) as a system to represent **inner** and **external** reality, the point of difference remains: whether language is psychologically constructed by the individual (Piaget & Inhelder, 1969), or socially constructed through interaction with others (Vygotsky, 1978). According to a DSP, this is a moot point because cognitive constructivism and social constructivism are complementary processes.

A dynamic system perspective

Human development is concerned with growth and change transitions; it is about creating something more from something less (van Geert, 2019). There is general conformity in human development, and at the same time, there is individual uniqueness. A DSP offers a general framework to reconcile different viewpoints to converge on the principle of self-organisation. Self-organisation refers to the emergence of order. A transition phase marks a period of reorganisation, where old patterns break down and new ones appear before a new level of order emerges. During a transition phase, growth and change are strongly influenced by even small effects.

A dynamic system is a formal system where the current state of being depends on the previous or initial state; expressed simply as the next state of organisation equals the product of the initial state, resources, and time. Resources are deemed to be whatever is needed to get to the next state:

[Initial State X (Resources + Time) = Next State]

Through an iterative process, the next state becomes the initial (present) state, and so on. In a dynamic system, the current state generates its successive state by a principle of change. The acquisition of written language by the end of Year 1 (next state) is the product of external and internal influences for written language attained, or not, from birth to school entry (initial state) with external contingent instruction and internal processes (resources) plus maturation (time). Resources consist of components that exert specific forces upon one another and by doing so, change each others' and their own properties.

No theory of development provides an adequate explanation of what starts off the developmental process. From a DSP, it is assumed that causal factors driving development lie in the developmental process itself. New development arises from processes that drive 'being developed' or drive self-organisation. The archetypical example of self-organisation is the human embryo. Self-organisation is when the order and structure of the system emerge from the coordination of local relationships between multiple elements.

Development from a DSP is not restricted to ages and stages commonly found in developmental psychology although ages and stages are accommodated within a DSP framework. Fundamental to a DSP is the tenet that developing humans are complex systems composed of individual elements, embedded within, and open to, a complex environment. Each new level of organisation is characterised by phase or transition states and may be preceded by discontinuities or increased variability. As a result, cross-sectional studies often fail to capture the 'messiness' of development. Pre-school children will mix identifiable letters with scribbles and yet claim to be able to read both equally well. On the one hand, they have understood the significance of letters for reading, but on the other hand, they are yet unable to distinguish between modes of notation.

In a dynamic system, change may be non-linear depending on the sensitivity, or lack of sensitivity, to initial states. Large changes in the system can be generated by small differences in current conditions. For example, the nature and timing of school instruction can lead to large changes in the system, depending on the initial state. In the context of written language development, we can imagine that at any one time, there is an initial state for motor, language, perceptual and cognitive elements upon which instruction impacts. If initial states differ slightly, they will converge – if they are widely different, they may diverge.

Both Piaget and Vygotsky proposed dual mechanisms of change that were coupled together.

Piaget's dual mechanisms of **assimilation**, interpreting new experiences by drawing on existing structures without changing them, and **accommodation**, changing or transforming existing structures to incorporate new experiences, reflect an internal dynamic mechanism of change.

Vygotsky described the dynamic of development as a 'spiral passing through the same point while advancing to a higher level' by means of a dual mechanism, internalisation, which is the **internal** reconstruction of an **external** operation that occurs in the **zone of proximal development**. The zone of proximal development is defined as the distance between actual development and potential development that is possible under adult guidance or in collaboration with capable peers.

Neuroimaging provides evidence for coupled mechanisms to build the structure of written language. The individual contributes to structure by active visual engagement with print, handwriting and handling 3D letters (James & Engelhardt, 2012). The socio-cultural environment contributes to structure using print exposure and contingent responses to individuals' engagement with written language.

The importance of the transition phase

What is helpful about reframing child development from a DSP perspective is the concept of a transition phase. As stated several times in this book, the vast majority of children acquire written language between the ages of four to seven years, which is almost half a lifetime in the life of a seven-year-old child. Yet, we can underestimate the length of time needed for the transition phase, especially when we compare younger children with older children in the same classroom cohort. All children need time and resources to acquire H2H skills, but some may need additional scaffolding to do so. If it is acknowledged that the transition phase may take longer than expected, then it is also time to review resources. Provide additional small group instruction for children who need it, earlier rather than later. In a dynamic system, during the transition phase, small effects can strongly influence growth and change.

Variability
The other insight of the DSP is that of variability, or the messiness, of development. When children are learning to handwrite they demonstrate considerable variability. This is to be expected, but with

instruction, practice, feedback and self-evaluation, the variability decreases. Nonetheless, it is important not to accept variability as inevitable. Formative comparison and ranking between children are helpful to determine targeted practice sessions for problem letters. The messy transition phase encompasses jumps, progressions and declines, but overall, the trend is upward toward mastery. A test for mastery (consolidation) is when the system, orthographic code and graphomotor plan, are able to withstand perturbation or disturbance; the child can read unfamiliar decodable words without reference to pictures and independently retrieve and reproduce letters without visual reference to the alphabet.

In summary

This chapter presented an overview of a dynamic system perspective for understanding how children come to acquire written language. The child actively constructs a conceptual understanding of written language knowledge, and the society around him actively supports the child's written language knowledge construction.

The chapter highlighted the importance of the initial state upon which time (Foundation Year and Year 1) and resources (explicit, systematic instruction and monitored practice) act for children to move to the next state of stability, that is, written language acquisition. Variability is information during the transition phase and serves to modify and differentiate instruction.

The next chapter follows on from the idea of different initial states in body systems that need to integrate dynamically to support written language acquisition.

CHAPTER 11

The Integration of Parts

What children know about handwriting is related to what they know about the general system of written language.
Ferreiro & Teberosky, 1979

Effective teachers exploit the clear overlap between writing, reading, spelling, and sentence construction.
Berninger, 2007

Written language is complex. It has a long incubation period, even for those steeped in print-rich environments. To acquire written language, you need to have the orthographic code and the graphomotor plan. Most children read before they write, so their ability to handwrite is an insight into their understanding of the written language system.

It may seem self-evident, but the question of 'what is handwriting' attracts various explanations. Handwriting is: a multi-component task (van Galen, 1991); a linguistic act (Abbott & Berninger, 1993); a psychomotor skill that is developed by instruction (Hamstra-Bletz & Blote, 1993); a complex skill encompassing visual motor coordination, cognitive and perceptual skills, as well as tactile and kinaesthetic sensitivities (Feder, Majnemer, & Synnes, 2000); a form of language production that like speech involves different processing stages (Soler Vilageliu & Kandel, 2012); a mechanical skill (Rubin & Henderson, 1982); a complex human activity that appears to be an outward manifestation of the individual's perceptual-motor abilities (Rosenblum, Weiss, & Parush, 2003); and a perceptual motor skill (Furner, 1969).

From the point of view of the framework, the integration of these contributors to handwriting – motor, cognitive, linguistic and perceptual systems – act as influences. Occupational therapists call these influences **performance components** for handwriting (Feder & Majnemer, 2007). Each of these systems may be at a different (initial) state if viewed from a DSP. These systems are body/brain influences that can either facilitate or detract from written language acquisition. Therefore, time spent on 'body work' is not wasted. Fine motor activities to support fine motor development are helpful. Commercially available programmes such as Brain Gym, EduDance, EduYoga, Move to Learn and Primary Movement helps children understand location terms such as middle, top, down, up and across in their bodies. Location terms are used when describing the spatial parameters of letter strokes. Bodywork is important for posture and primes children to attend and so benefit from instruction and apply themselves to attain the orthographic code and graphomotor plan.

What can we do to bring it all together?

Differentiate instruction
It has been documented that approximately 25% of children enter school with at least one developmental vulnerability. These children are likely to need additional support earlier rather than later. The remaining 75% can be further divided into those who will experience no difficulties acquiring written language to those who may take a bit longer or require additional monitoring. Early intervention is always best. Differentiated instruction in small groups is routine in most classrooms and often effects positive change.

Early differentiated instruction resonates with the third characteristic nominated by Paris (2005), that of **universality**. Children demonstrate considerable variability in literacy development when they enter school. Nevertheless, effective educators expect children to learn to read and write and the goal is to narrow the distribution of constrained skills. Effective educators reduce inter-child, and intra-child, variability during the acquisition of universally mastered skills.

Reduce variability
As previously stated, the aim during the transition phase is to reduce variability. At the same time, variability is information that can help to inform instruction. Direct instruction that uses an 'I do, We do, You do' approach can be made more explicit to the children, so they can engage with setting small goals for themselves. Children are agents in their learning, so setting small goals and achieving them supports a growth mindset.

What you do and when you do it matters
Highly explicit, systematic phonics instruction is necessary to acquire the orthographic code. Highly explicit, systematic instruction in

letter formation is necessary to acquire the graphomotor plan. But when, and how it is delivered can make a difference. Gaps in alphabet knowledge need to be addressed earlier rather than later. Sensory motor approaches are more effective for younger students, after which cognitive strategies become more effective.

This book has emphasised the H2H skills, but H2G skills are being taught across the same time, for example, comprehension, text structure, telling a story or recounting. There is great overlap for the acquisition of these skills during the transition phase, and instruction in H2G skills helps to integrate H2H skills. However, because H2G skills are the desired product of H2H skills they are more valued. This can lead to confusion about what is more important. What happens in Foundation and Year 1 has an enormous impact on what happens to academic performance after that. What you teach depends on when (Suggate, 2010).

What are some principles I can follow?

What should be obvious by now, is that there is no one way to teach children to read or to handwrite. Yet, to acquire written language, children must have the orthographic code and the graphomotor plan in LTM. There are many different programmes, but the general principles to follow include: instructing, monitoring, evaluating and maintaining achieved performance. How these are realised is in the dynamic relationship between educator and child.

> *Children can only provide evidence in the form of what they write, make, do, and say. All cognitive and affective learning is inferred from these four observable actions.*
> **Griffin, 2010**

The Integration of Parts

In summary

This chapter presented a brief overview of what occupational therapists call performance components that support integration of body/brain influences. As the different descriptions of handwriting highlight, the ability to handwrite is positively correlated with motor, cognitive, linguistic and perceptual skills. Therefore, developing these skills should not be neglected, but rather regarded as an adjunct to instruction in the orthographic code and graphomotor plan.

Positive correlations between the home environment and written language acquisition are well-known and encouraged by health and community services from birth. It is not one thing but many things that contribute to the integration of knowledge, skills and abilities, for children to learn to read and write.

The final chapter acknowledges that readers want to make a difference in children's lives.

CHAPTER 12

The Desire to Make a Difference

Written word processing starts in our eyes. Only the centre of the retina, called the fovea, has a fine enough resolution to allow for the recognition of small print. Our gaze must therefore move around the page constantly Whenever our eyes stop, we only recognise one or two words. Each of them is then split up into myriad fragments by retinal neutrons and must be put back together before it can be recognised. Our visual system progressively extracts graphemes, syllables, prefixes, suffixes and word roots. Two major parallel processing routes eventually come into play: the phonological route, which converts letters into speech sounds, and the lexical route, which gives access to a mental dictionary of word meanings.
Dehaene, 2009

Acquiring written language is hard work, but the rewards are great. Some children have to work harder and take longer than others, but with support, they can achieve. We want to make a difference – that is why we are involved with helping children read and write. Helen Keller was blind and deaf, but her teacher Anne Sullivan helped her to crack the mapping code, mediated by touch, between the world and language. At some time, we all needed to crack the code to read and write. This chapter summarises a few recommendations made throughout the book.

Work on constrained skills during the transition phase

There are critical periods in human development when it is easier to achieve a skill than when you need to acquire it later. For example, most professional classical musicians come from musical families. They were exposed to hearing classical music probably in the womb, saw adults perform with musical instruments and were instructed in learning to play one or more instruments themselves. However, it does not mean that as an adult, without the benefit of a classical musical family, you will not be able to learn to play a musical instrument. All that can be said is that it will probably take more time and effort than if you had learnt as a young child surrounded by players of, and instructors in, classical music. The same may be said for learning another language other than your mother tongue. Most fluent bilingual or trilingual speakers were exposed to these oral languages from a very early age. Some adults enjoy learning new languages, but they need to work harder at the pronunciation of the target language than native speakers.

It has been highlighted that there is a development progression to learning to read and write. Just as the baby from a classical musical family does not start playing Mozart as soon as they can sit upright (there may always be an exception), so most children do not begin reading and writing words until their fourth year, although the exception might. The critical period for learning to read and write is generally considered to be between the ages of four to seven years. That is, over a period of three years we can expect that children will attain the H2H skills as the foundation for their literacy growth. It is often around age four to seven years that children who have been immersed in music or a different language are distinguished from their peers in the musical facility and bilingual fluency.

The critical period is often interpreted ideologically. Some authorities say you should start as early as possible and begin formal instruction at the age of four years; others say that children need more exposure to activities that facilitate acquiring H2H skills and begin formal instruction later. The Play Curriculum, the Developmental Curriculum, the School Readiness approach and the Montessori School Approach express different views on how the developmental continuum is perceived.

There are three things to say about the critical period between four and seven years. One is that children have had at least four years immersed in environments that primed them for formal instruction. Second, the critical period is approximately three years so that is almost half a lifetime of a seven-year-old child. Third, educators have time to be sensitive to individual developmental differences to modify the pace of instruction.

Counterintuitively, what seems like a long time at age four years is minimal over the life span. Given this expanse of time, there is ample opportunity for children to attain H2H skills as a foundation for H2G skills. Paris (2005) compares H2H skills to ceiling skills. Once you know them, you do not get better at knowing them; rather, you only get better at manipulating what you know to grow other literacy abilities. That is exciting for both educators and children.

However well-informed and committed educators are, they are limited in their resolve if children do not attend school. Poor school attendance is a major predictor of academic failure. The reasons for poor school attendance are complex and beyond the scope of this book. Marginalised groups are over-represented in the data for poor school attendance. Much hand-wringing and demands for change appear to make little difference. Some serious rethink is warranted in this area at each level of the ecological systems that surround children who do not attend school.

Appreciate the developmental nature of learning

It is necessary to appreciate the developmental nature of learning in general and of handwriting in particular. Many years ago in the 1930s, a teacher, Mrs Hildreth, began observing children in four different classrooms. She continued this observational study over a period of two years. Every nine months the children were subjected to a battery of tests copying shapes, numbers and letters, as well as writing numbers and letters to dictation. At the end of the study, she had this to say (Hildreth, 1932):

> *During the period between the ages of approximately four and seven the subjects of the experiment progressed from a stage of learning that was vague, confused and incoherent, to a stage of maximum clarity and ease of accomplishment. The excessive squirming and superfluous large muscle movements, the indecision, failure, enormous struggle and discouragement of the youngest pupils had disappeared by the time of the end test and had given*

place to orderly workmanship with ease of accomplishment in which superfluous movements had been reduced to a minimum in which the child clearly showed in his total behaviour, his familiarity with the task, his success with it and his delight in it.

This is what mastery looks like, and it feels good. Children delight in their abilities! What if someone has labelled the vague, confused squirmer as having 'problems' before they had time to perform the final test? Instead, Hildreth recognised that learning is hard work; the reward comes from surviving the struggle. Hildreth was only an observer; it was educator support and judicial scaffolding that helped these children achieve this amazing milestone.

The early years are characterised by dramatic advancements in some areas, gradual evolving capabilities in others, and plateaus or even declines in development. There may be a growth spurt in number concepts, which then plateaus, followed by a growth spurt in drawings and attempts at writing names. This 'messy' developmental period is not unusual for many children. Unfortunately, there may be too much pressure to move on before children have consolidated their H2H skills. Frequent use of dynamic monitoring, watching children as they form their letters, and retrieval practice to verify knowledge of foundation concepts will help.

Learning to handwrite is hard work

Learning to handwrite legibly is hard work and that's why most children don't like doing it. But like the hero of the universal story, they come out changed for the better in the end (see Hildreth). Children must practise handwriting letterforms, but drill to skill in blocked practice (e.g. 45 minutes once a week) is probably not the most effective way. It is better to have shorter, but more frequent sessions. Commercial handwriting books that are used as a substitute for handwriting instruction can act as a detractor influence because children trace or copy letters without sufficient cognitive engagement to build the cognitive architecture that enables independent retrieval of letterforms. Explicit instruction from an informed educator is always best.

It is essential to include handwriting practice in any handwriting intervention and it is estimated that children need at least 20 hours of handwriting instruction (Hoy, Egan, & Feder, 2011); some children may need more. Because graphomotor plan as described in this book is a constrained skill, some children will achieve reading and handwriting before others in the same class. Monitoring and maintenance replace instruction for these proficient children. However, intermittent review of 'problem' letters will always remain relevant.

In summary

This chapter reinforced the idea that acquiring written language is hard work: for the child and the educator. Very few children learn to read and write without adult instruction. It can be challenging and time-consuming on many levels but the rewards are great for the child, society and the educator. Continual reflection on our practice, collaborating with other educators, and consulting with specialist services when necessary are available means to support us on our journey to make a difference in the literacy lives of children.

Afterword

I hope you enjoyed reading *Begin it Write* and that it has stimulated your thinking about how children acquire early written language.

My thinking and reading has led me to conclude that children cannot do without the orthographic code and graphomotor plan if they are to learn to read and write. These two skills are necessary for all that follows, and direct instruction is necessary to achieve them.

The impetus for the book was preceded by my PhD study examining the impact of cognitive load on handwriting legibility in Year 1 and Year 2 children. Cognitive load is often cited as a reason for poor handwriting and I agree with this proposition. However, it niggled me that cognitive load can hardly be used as an explanation for beginner writers who have not learnt to handwrite. Why have they not learnt to handwrite given that they had all received instruction? In *Begin it Write*, I offer a framework to dissect what the contributing factors might be.

My intention is to follow *Begin it Write* with a second book *Keeping it Write*, which is based on the findings of my PhD study. To examine the impact of cognitive load on legibility when children are learning to handwrite, I needed to devise an instrument to measure legibility. Precise handwriting measurement of self-generated connected text during periods of considerable variability, when children are still learning to handwrite, is time consuming and has limited value. So, what did I do?

Keeping it Write will explore legibility measurement in early years. It will also explore in more detail the role of *Influences: The Body & Brain I Inhabit* from the point of view of detractor influence and how differentiated instruction can help children acquire written language.

Author Bio

Cornelia Staats is an experienced paediatric occupational therapist, who, over her 30-year career has worked in the public, private and university sector. She is committed to supporting children's participation, with peers and caregivers, in what they need to do, and what they want to do. Cornelia has benefited from extensive training and collaboration with other professionals in the health and education space. Taking her lead from the children and families with whom she has worked, Cornelia has modified her practice over time to take a more comprehensive view of written language as it relates to everyday school occupations such as reading and writing. This book is the result of her current thinking and her approach to targeting handwriting referrals. When she is not working, she is walking, swimming, cycling or riding her motorbike.

Resources

These free resources are available
at www.corriestaats.com

Alphabet Games
- The importance of learning the alphabet cannot be overstated. These games can easily be adopted in the home. Educators are creative people and the listed ideas will no doubt generate many more fun games!

Universal Shapes
- The eight universal shapes for lower-case letters.
- The four universal shapes for upper-case letters.
- These shapes form the basis for the symbols that we know as the alphabet. They are configured according to the characteristic features that identifies the letter. Cursive script uses entry and exit strokes.

Verbal Cues
- The verbal cues that accompany the universal shapes for lower-case letters. Some alternative cues are offered to demonstrate that verbal cues, in themselves, are not prescriptive, but rather make sense to the educator and/or children. What is important is that there is consistency in using the verbal cue when demonstrating, and monitoring, letter formations.
- The verbal cues that accompany the universal shapes for upper-case letters.

Online Learning Modules
Begin it Write

The 12 self-directed learning modules are aligned to the book, but each explores objections that may be raised by the presented material, and a possible response.

Each module invites the learner to reflect on their own experience, knowledge and practice to articulate their personal theory of written language development. Becoming conscious of our beliefs and bias helps us become better educators. Many roads lead to Rome; there is no single programme that will give all the answers, but different approaches have different effects on children's learning. What matters is what you do when, and why.

Each module presents a video tutorial and is accompanied by a module workbook. The modules can be purchased separately or as the entire 12-module learning course. Please register your interest at www.corriestaats.com

The modules are:
- The Future Scene
- The Current Scene
- The Framework
- The Have to Have
- The Orthographic Code
- The Graphomotor Plan
- The Influences on Have to Have
- The Environment in Which I Live
- The Body and Brain I Inhabit
- The Dynamic System Perspective
- The Integration of Parts
- The Desire to Make a Difference

Resources

Workshop Presentation
Begin it Write

Cornelia Staats PhD, MEd, MHthSc(OT), GradDipEd, BAppSc(OT) is an experienced paediatric occupational therapist, who, over her 30-year career has worked in the public, private and university sector.

The book, *Begin it Write*, grew from her current thinking and approach to handwriting/fine motor referrals. Over her 30-year career, she has encountered several methods for addressing written language concerns; some of which have come full circle. For children to acquire written language they must have the orthographic code and graphomotor plan. In addition the role of influences must be considered; their role cannot be underestimated to Begin it Write. Based on her book, Cornelia has designed a full day workshop that can be modified according to allocated time and format.

The workshop is divided into four sessions. It can be adapted to suit the requesting educator group audience. Each section is accompanied by practical exercises and time for discussion in small groups. A workbook is available of the presentation notes.

First, the role of influences is examined and our beliefs about how they impact, or not, the initial state of the child's dynamic system for instruction.

Second, the role of Have-to-Have skills are reviewed and our beliefs about how they are acquired. There will be time for participants to challenge the model and articulate their rationale for doing so.

Third, practical strategies to acquire the Have-to-Have skills will be discussed. Participants will consider available resources in their locale and how they can be utilised more effectively.

The final session will conclude with establishing the distinction between Have-to-Have skills and the Have-to-Grow skills, at the same time, identifying how their overlap is important. Participants will leave the workshop, confident and secure in their knowledge they can make a difference in the lives of children to acquire written language, and can articulate why they are able to do so.

To enquire about Cornelia's availability to speak at your venue or event please contact www.corriestaats.com

Appendix 1

TERM	DEFINITIONS & EXPLANATIONS
Acrophonic Principle	the letter name corresponds to the letter sound; this can be for initial phonemes (consonant-vowel names) e.g. b[ee], d, p, or as a final phoneme (vowel-consonant name) e.g. [e]f, l, m, n, r, s
Alphabet Knowledge	letter shape, name, sound and sequence
Alphabetic Principle	conceptual understanding that letters and letter patterns represent the sounds of spoken language; in order to retrieve pronunciation for unfamiliar word/s (mat, ten, stop) children access systematic letter-sound relationships
Cognitive Architecture	long-term memory and working memory
Cognitive constructivism	knowledge is biologically constructed
Concepts of print	direction of print and return sweep, spaces between words, text read left to right and from top to bottom

Decode	a process by which the reader uses knowledge of the relationship between letters and sounds to work out how to sound out letters and read written words
Detractor Influence	environmental, brain and body factors that make it more difficult to acquire written language
Digraph	two letters represent a single sound; there are vowel digraphs e.g. ai, ea, and consonant digraphs e.g. sh, ph as well as vowel/consonant digraphs e.g. er, ow.
Dynamic Systems Perspective	theoretical perspective that development is about change; context and time are critical aspects of development and performance; change is produced from the interaction of multiple subsystems within the person, task and environment; all subsystems potentially contribute to emerging behaviour
Dyslexia	learning disorder characterised by difficulty reading; problem with conversion of written symbols into speech sounds
Facilitator Influence	environmental, brain and body factors that make it easier to acquire written language
Foundation Year	first year of compulsory school in Australia; it is known by a variety of names in different Australian States (e.g. kindergarten, preparatory, reception, pre-primary)
Grapheme	a letter or group of letters that represent a phoneme in a word e.g. /f/ in fog; /ph/ in phone

Appendix 1

Graphomotor Plan	the accuracy and preciseness of letterform as mental representations, recalled from memory, retrieval of stable motor plan to independently reproduce individual letters adhering to characteristic spatial parameters
Handwriting	the independent recall and legible production of all 26 alphabet letters in upper case, and in lower case
Influences	factors that either make it easier or more difficult to acquire written language
Long-term Memory	unlimited information storage capacity that can be maintained for life/long periods in contrast to working memory which persists for seconds to minutes
Mastery	passing the threshold from not reading and handwriting to attaining the above; cognitive structural change has taken place
Neurodiversity	umbrella term to describe person differences from so-called 'typical' brain processes that affects learning and behaviour
Neurotypical	umbrella term to describe so-called 'typical' brain processes relating to learning and behaviour
Orthographic Code	a broad concept that relates to alphabet knowledge and independent use of the alphabetic principle to decode and blend phonemes in text
Phoneme	the smallest unit of sound in a word e.g. cat has three phonemes /c/, /a/, /t/ and the word shop also has three phonemes /sh/, /o/, /p/

Phonemic Awareness	ability to hear, identify and manipulate individual phonemes in a word (segment, blend, deletion, substitution)
Phonic knowledge	ability to map the relationship between alphabet letters and sounds they represent; identify and manipulate sounds, blending phonemes to form/read (at least) one syllable words
Phonological awareness	broad concept that relates to sounds/rhythms of the language. It includes hearing and identifying rhymes, syllables and onset/rime
Rasch Model	a mathematical model that examines the relationship between latent traits (unobserved attributes) and their manifestations (observed performance); success on tested items is determined by personal ability and item difficulty; Rasch analysis is a confirmatory model because the data must meet Rasch model requirements to form a measurement scale (data must fit the model)
Reading	ability to decode and synthesise (blend) at least three phonemes to read as a word
Social constructivism	knowledge is socially constructed
Word knowledge	identify and manipulate sounds, blending phonemes to form one syllable words; know how to read and write some high-frequency and consonant vowel consonant words (CVC), know how to write their own name

Appendix 1

Working Memory	limited information storage capacity to hold and use information in the execution of cognitive tasks; execution is faster if information elements are chunked from LTM rather than processed as individual elements
Written language	learning to read, and learning to handwrite text; the trajectory of children's acquisition of written language show similarities to the history of written language as a cultural phenomenon
Year 1	the year after Foundation Year

Appendix 2

ABBREVIATION	DESCRIPTION
AC	Australian Curriculum
ADHD	Attention Deficit Hyperactivity Disorder
AEDC	Australian Early Development Census
AEDI	Australian Early Development Index
ASD	Autism Spectrum Disorder
AT	Alphabet task
COVID	Coronavirus Disease of 2019
DCD	Developmental Coordination Disorder
DI	Detractor Influences
EAK	Enhanced Alphabet Knowledge
EPPE	Effective Provision of Preschool Education
FI	Facilitator Influences
FY	Foundation Year
GP	Graphomotor Plan
H2G	Have to Grow
H2H	Have to Have

LTM	Long-term Memory
MOOC	Massive Open Online Course
NAPLAN	National Assessment Program for Literacy and Numeracy
OC	Orthographic Code
OECD	Organisation for Economic Co-operation and Development
PISA	Program for International Student Assessment
RM	Rasch Model
SPD	Sensory Processing Disorder
SRSD	Self-Regulated Strategy Development
T2	Term 2
T4W	Talk for Writing
USA	United States of America
WM	Working Memory
Y1	Year 1

Appendix 3

A conservative time line for consolidation of the graphomotor plan

	FY-Term 1	FY-T2	FY-T3	FY-T4	Y1-Term 1	Y1-Term 2	Y1-Term 3	Y1-Term 4
	Alphabet knowledge in recursive cycles; including demonstration of how to write the letters; dance and clapping/rapping games to rhymes and rhythm; play print games e.g. 'write' letters to post, message in card to caregiver, alphabet jumping games; spot the letter '?' amongst different fonts and cases; snap game with alphabet pack of upper- and lower-case letters; alphabet name tally of children in class				Review alphabet knowledge; letter recognition, name and sound; **Alphabet Task** (independent retrieval for reproducing letters) as baseline; review; to inform targeted intervention **Goal free** – 'write all the letters you know' (T1) **Dictated alphabet** – dictate, random and/or in sequence, all letters of the alphabet (T2,T3) **Standard Alphabet Task** – children independently retrieve and write out the letters of the alphabet, in order, in lowercase (allow two minutes end T2 and allow one minute beginning T4, children to write alphabet again if they finish before allotted time)			
		First round of formal, explicit instruction for handwritten upper-case letters (and name & sound); sensory motor approaches; write out CVC words e.g. CAT, MOP	First round of formal, explicit instruction for handwritten lower-case letters (and name & sound); sensory motor approaches: write out CVC words e.g. cat, mop	First round of formal, explicit instruction for handwritten lower-case letters (and name & sound); sensory motor approaches; evaluation to model; memorise verbal cues; children set mini goals; targeted practice to achieve goal	Review of upper-case letters	Monitor and review as indicated	Second round of formal, explicit instruction lower-case letters; standard lined or dotted third paper; cognitive approaches, e.g. model letter; self-evaluation to model; memorise verbal cues; children set mini goals; targeted practice to achieve goal	Third round of formal review/repair lower-case letters writing words and sentences in dictated and self-generated text; dotted third paper; attend to size and spacing; cognitive approaches e.g. self-evaluation to model; memorise verbal cues; children set mini goals; targeted practice to achieve goal
							Dictated words and sentences emphasising space between words; begin with capital (upper-case) letter, end with full stop	
	Integrate with activities of selected phonics programme (extended phonics is considered H2G in the context of this framework)							
	Integrate with language, literacy and literature curriculum (AC) activities (H2G): Educator read aloud narrative and information text for children to enjoy and to increase concepts of print and vocabulary exposure (H2G)							
	Writing Programme (H2G): e.g. Self-Regulated Strategy Development (SRSD); Talk for Writing (T4W)							

Bibliography

Abbott, R. D., & Berninger, V. (1993). Structural equation modeling of relationships among developmental skills and writing skills in primary- and intermediate-grade writers. *Journal of Educational Psychology, 85*(3), 478-508.

Abbott, R. D., Berninger, V., & Fayol, M. (2010). Longitudinal relationship of levels of language in writing and between writing and reading in grade 1-7 . *Journal of Educational Psychology, 102*, 281-298.

ACRA, A. C. (2022). *NAPLAN National Report for 2022*. Sydney: ACARA.

AEDC. (2021). 2021 AEDC National Report Retrieved from www.aedc.gov.au

Baddeley, A. D. & Hitch, G. J. (1974). Working memory. In G. A. Bower, *Recent Advances in Learning and Motivation* (Vol.8, pp. 47-89). New York: Academic Press.

Baddeley, A. D., Hitch, G., & Allen, R. (2019). From short-term store to multicomponent working memory: The role of the modal model. *Memory & Cognition, 47*, 575-588.

Bara, F., & Gentaz, E. (2011). Haptics in teaching handwriting: The role of perceptual and visuo-motor skills. *Human Movement Science, 30*(4), 745-759.

Bear, D. R. (2008). *Words their way: Word study for phonics, vocabulary and spelling instruction (4th ed.)*. New Jersey: Pearson Education .

Beery, K. E. (1997). *The developmental test of visual-motor integration (4th ed.)*. Cleveland: Modern Curricumlum Press.

Berninger, V. G. (1997). Treatment of handwriting problems in beginning writers: Transfer from handwriting to composition. *Journal of Educational Psychology, 89*(4), 652-666.

Bialystok, E. (1995). Making concepts of print symbolic: Understanding how writing represents language. *First language , 15*(45), 317-338.

Bonnor, C. K. (2021). *Structural failure: Why Australia keeps falling short of our educational goals*. Sydney: UNSW Gonski Institute.

Bronfenbrenner, U. (1986). Ecology of the family as a context for human development: Research perspectives. *Developmental Psychology, 22*(6), 723-742.

Capodieci, A. L. (2018). Handwriting difficulties in children with attention deficit hyperactivity disorder (ADHD). *Research in developmental disabilites, 74*, 41-49.

Changizi, M. A. (2006). The structure of letters and symbols throughout human history are selected to match those found in objects in natural scenes. *American Naturalist, 167*(5), 117-139.

Colheart, M. (2017). What kind of things cause children's reading difficulties? *Australian Journal of Learning Difficulties, 20*(2), 103-112.

Dehaene, S. (2009). *Reading in the brain.* New York: Viking.

Dewey, C., Fleming, P., & Golding, J. (1998). Does the supine sleeping position have any adverse effect on the child? *Pediatrics, 101*(1), 1-5.

Drane, C. V. (2020). The impact of learning at home on the education outcomes of vulnerable children in Australia during the COVID-19 pandemic. Literature Review prepared by the National Centre for Student Equity in Higher Education, Curtin University, Australia.

Drouin, M. H. (2012). Alphabet knowledge in preschool: A Rasch model analysis. *Early Chldhoold Research Quarterly, 27*(3), 543-554.

Dunn, W. (. (1991). *Pediatric Occupational Therapy.* Thorofare, NJ: Slack Inc.

Feder, K. P., & Majnemer, A. (2007). Handwriting development, compentency, and intervention. *Developmental Medicine & Child Neurology, 49*(4), 312-317.

Feder, K., Majnemer, A., & Synnes, A. (2000). Handwriting: current trends in occupational therapy practice. *Canadian Journal of Occupational Therapy, 67*(3), 197-204.

Foulin, J. N. (2005). Why is letter name knowledge such a good predictor of learning to read? *Reading and Writing,* 18, 129-155.

Fromkin, V. R. (1990). *An introduction to language.* Sydney: Holt, Rinehart & Winston.

Furner, B. A. (1969). The perceptual-motor nature of learning to handwrite. *Elementary English, 46*(7), 886-894.

Gathercole, S., & Alloway, T. (2008). *Working memory and learning.* London: Sage.

Hamstra-Bletz, L., & Blote, A. (1993). A longitudinal study on dysgraphic handwriting in primary school. *Journal of Learning Difficulties, 26*(10), 689-699.

Handle, H. C. (2022). Handwriting in Autism Spectrum Disorder: A Literature Review. *NeuroSci, 3*(4), 558-565.

Hattie, J., & Zierer, K. (2019). *Visible learning insights.* New York: Routledge.

Hickey, C. (2021, December). *The Conversation.* Retrieved 2022, from https://theconversation.com/a-crowded-curriculum-sure-it-may-be-complex-but-so-is-the-world-kids-must-engage-with

Hildreth, G. (1932). The success of young children in number and letter construction. *Child Development, 3*(1), 1-14.

Hoy, M., Egan, M., & Feder, K. (2011). A systematic review of interventions to improve handwriiting. *Canadian Journal of Occupational Therapy,* 78, 13-25.

James, K. H. (2010). Sensori-motor experience leads to changes in visual processing in the developing brain. *Developmental Science, 13*(2), 279-288.

James, K., & Engelhardt, L. (2012). The effects of handwriting experience on function brain development in pre-literate children. *Trends in Neuroscience and Education,* 1, 32-42.

Bibliography

Jones, C. D. (2012). Enhanced alphabet knowledge instruction: Exploring a change of frequency, focus, and distributed cycles of review. *Reading Psychology, 33*, 448-464.

Juel, C. (1988). Learning to read and write: A longitudinal study of 54 children from first to fourth grade. *Journal of Educational Psychology, 80*(4), 437-447.

Katusic, S. K. (2009). The forgotten learning disability: Epidemiology of written-language disorder in a population-based birth cohort (1976-1982), Rochester, Minnesota. *Paediatrics, 123*(5), 1306-1313.

Keating, D. P. (2007). Formative evaluation of the early development instrument: Progress and prospects. *Early Education and Development, 18*(3), 561-570.

Lamb, S. H. (2020). *Educational opportunity in Australia 2020: Who succeeds and who misses out.* Centre for International Research on Education Systems. Melbourne: Victoria University for the Mitchell Institute.

Lamb, S., & Huo, S. (2017). *Counting the costs of lost opportunity in Australian education.* Mitchell Institute Report No.02/2017. Melbourne. Retrieved November 2021, from www.mitchellinstitute.org.au DOI: 10.4226/80/591e74a01d950

Lego, P. (1983). *The art of handwriting: Perfecting the foundation skills through only seven movements.* Cammeray NSW: Martin Educational.

Lewis, M. D. (2000). The promise of dynamic systems approaches for an integrated account of human development. *Child Development, 71*(1), 36-43.

Louden, W., Rohl, M., Barrett Pugh, C., Brown, C., Cairney, T., & Elderfield, J. (2005). *In teacher's hands: Effective literacy teaching practices in the early years of schooling.* Perth: Edith Cowan University: Australian Government Department of Education, Science and Training.

Marr, D., & Cermak, S. (2002). Predicting handwriting performance of early elementary students with the developmental test of visual-motor integration. *Perceptual Motor Skills, 95*(2), 661-669.

Martlew, M., & Sorsby, A. (1994). Functional graphic representation: Pictures and symbols. In C., Faure, P., Keuss, G., Lorette, & A., Vinter, *Advances in handwriting and drawing: A multidisciplinary approach.* Paris: Europa.

McCarthy, L. (1977). A child learns the alphabet. *Visible Language, 11*(3), 271-284.

Neuman, S. B. (2006). N is for nonsensical: Low-income preschool children need content-rich instuction, not drill in procedural skills. *Educational Leadership, 64*, 28-31.

OECD. (2015). *Students, Computers and Learning: Making the Connection.* Paris, France.

OECD. (2018). *www.oecd.org.* Retrieved from PISA 2018: www.oecd.org

Olsen, J. Z. (1998). *Handwriting without tears.* MD: Author.

Overvelde, A. (2013). *Which practice makes perfect? Experimental studies on the acquisition of movement sequences to identify the best learning condition in good and poor writers.* Retrieved from http://repository.ubn.ru.nl/bitstream/handle/2066/116781/116781.pdf.

Palmis, S., Velay, J., Habib, M., Anton, J., Nazarian, B., Sein, J., & Longcamp, M. (2021). The handwriting brain in middle childhood. *Developmental Science*, 24(2), e13046.

Paris, S. (2005). Reinterpreting the development of reading skills. *Reading Research Quarterly*, 40(2), 184-202.

Phillips, L. M., Norris, S., & Anderson, J. (2008). Unocking the door: is parents' reading to children the key to early literacy development? *Canadian Psychology*, 49(2), 81-88.

Piaget, J., & Inhelder, B. (1969). *The psychology of the child*. London: Routledge & Kegan Paul.

Piek, J., Dawson, L., Smith, L., & Gasson, N. (2008). The role of early fine and gross motor development on later motor and cognitive ability. *Human Movement Science*, 27(5), 668-681.

Puranik, C., & Lonigan, C. (2012). Name-writing proficiency, not length of name, is associated with preschool children's emergent literacy skills. *Early Childhood Research Quarterly*, 27(2), 284-294.

Puranik, C., Petscher, Y., & Lonigan, C. (2014). Learning to write letters: Examination of student and letter factors. *Journal of Experimental Child Psychology*, 128, 152-170.

Ray, K., Dally, K., Rowlandson, L., Tam, K., & Lane, A. E. (2022). The relationship of handwriting ability and literacy in kindergarten: A systematic review. *Reading and Writing*, 1119-1155.

Reutzel, D. R. (2015). Early literacy research: Findings primary-grade teachers will want to know. *The Reading Teacher*, 69(1), 14-24.

Rosenblum, S., Weiss, P., & Parush, S. (2003). Product and process evaluation of handwriting difficulties. *Educational Psychology Review*, 15(1), 41-81.

Rosenshine, B. (2012). Principles of instruction: Reserach-based strategies that all teachers should know. *The Education Digest*, 78(3), 30-40.

Rubin, N., & Henderson, S. (1982). Two sides of the same coin: variations in teaching methods and failure to learn to write. *Special Education: Forward Trends (Research Supplement)*, 9(4), 17-24.

Schneck, C. M. (1990). Descriptive analysis of the development progression of grip position for pencil and crayon control in nondysfunctional children. *American Journal of Occupational Therapy*, 44(10), 893-900.

Senechal, M., LeFevre, J-A., Thomas, E., & Daley, K. (1998). Differential effects of home literacy experiences on the development of oral and written language. *Reading Research Quarterly*, 33(1), 96-116.

Shanahan, T. (2006). Relations among oral language, reading, and writing development. In C. MacArthur, S. Graham, & J. Fitzgerald, *Handbook of writing research*. New York: Guildford Press.

Shaywitz, S. (2020). *Overcoming Dyslexia 2nd Edition*. US: Random House.

Simner, M. (1986). Further evidence on the relationship between form errors in preschool printing and early school achievement. In H. Kao, G. P. van

Galen, & R. Hossain, *Graphonomics: Contemporary research in handwriting.* Amsterdam: Elsevier

Soler Vilageliu, O., & Kandel, S. (2012). A longitudinal study of handwriting skills in pre-schoolers: The acquistion of syllable orientated programming strategies. *Reading and Writing, 25*(1), 151-162.

Staats, C. (2014). The impact of cognitive load on the aquisition of handwriting proficiency. *Unpublished PhD.* University of Western Australia.

Suggate, S. P. (2010). Why what we teach depends on when: Grade and reading intervention modality moderate effect size. *46*(6), 1556-1571.

Sylva, K., Melhuish, E., Sammons, P., Saraj-Blatchford, I., & Taggart, b. (2004). *The effective provision of preschool education (EPPE): Final Report.* Institute of Education, University of London: Department for Education and Skills/Sure Start.

Thelen, E., & Smith, L. (1994). *A dynamic system approach to the development of cognition and action.* Cambridge, Massachusetts: MIT Press.

Thompson, G. B. (2009). The long learning route to abstract letter units. *Cognitive Neuropsychology, 26*(1), 50-69.

Toffler, A. (1970). *Future shock.* New York: Random House.

Tooth, L. M. (2019). Adherence to screen time recommendations for Australian children aged 0-12. *Medical Journal of Australia, 211*(4), 181-182.

Treiman, R., & Kessler, B. (2004). The case of case: Children's knolwedge and use of upper- and lowercase letters. *Applied Psycholinguistics, 25*(3), 413-428.

van Galen, G. (1991). Handwriting issue for a psychomotor theory. *Human Movement Science, 10*(2-3), 165-191.

van Geert, P. (1994). *Dynamic systems of development: Change between complexity and chaos.* New York: Prentice Hall.

van Geert, P. (1998). A dynamic systems model of basic developmental meachanisms: Piaget, Vygotsky, and beyond. *Psychological Review, 105*(4), 634-677.

van Geert, P. (2019). Dynamic systems, process and development. *Human Development,* 63(3-4), 153-179.

Vygotsky, L. (1978). *Mind in Society: The development of higher psychological function.* Cambridge MA: Havard University Press.

Whitely, M. P. (2021). The effect of a child's relative age on numeracy and literacy test results: An analysis of NAPLAN in Western Australian government schools in 2017. *The Australian Educational Researcher, 48*(2), 249-265.

Zubrick, S., Taylor, C., & Christianson, D. (2015). Patterns and Predictors of Language and Literacy Abilities 4-10 Years in the Longitudinal Study of Australia. *PloS ONE, 10*(9), e0135612. doi:10.1371/journal.pone.0135612.

Zwicker, J., & Hadwin, A. (2009). Cognitive versus multisensory approaches to handwriting intervention: A randomised controlled trial. *OTJR: Occupation, Participation and Health, 29*(1), 40.

Notes

Begin It Write

Notes

Begin It Write

Notes

www.ingramcontent.com/pod-product-compliance
Lightning Source LLC
Chambersburg PA
CBHW030302100526
44590CB00012B/494